Professional Services Marketing
Strategy and Tactics

F. G. Crane, PhD

The Haworth Press
New York • London • Norwood (Australia)

The Haworth Press, Inc., 10 Alice Street, Binghamton, NY 13904-1580

Library of Congress Cataloging-in-Publication Data

Crane, F. G. (Frederick Gerard)
    Professional services marketing : strategy and tactics / F. G. Crane.
      p. cm.
    Includes bibliographical references and index.
    ISBN 1-56024-240-X (acid free paper).
    1. Professions – Marketing. I. Title.
HD8038.A1C73   1992
658.8'02 – dc20
                                                       91-36043
                                                          CIP

To My Family

ABOUT THE AUTHOR

F. G. Crane, PhD, is Professor of Marketing at Dalhousie University in Nova Scotia. He is also President of QMA Consulting Group Limited and has completed over 300 consulting assignments for service organizations worldwide. Dr. Crane is the author of over 70 publications including three books. He is currently the Editor of the *Journal of Promotion Management* published by The Haworth Press, Inc.

CONTENTS

Preface

The days when professionals could simply hang a shingle and wait for clients to beat a path to their door are long gone. Professionals must realize that their services, regardless of how good they are, simply do not sell themselves. Merely having the technical talent to supply a professional service does not mean that clients will patronize them. To many professionals, marketing is still a dirty word and the notion of marketing professional services is quickly dismissed. Others have reluctantly embraced some aspects of marketing, notably promotion, as a way to obtain a foothold in the market. Some professionals, however, have truly adopted a marketing orientation and have achieved rewarding results. They have also found that to be market driven is to be client driven. In essence, marketing is a business philosophy, a state of mind. It revolves around the central concepts of equitable exchange and client satisfaction. It begins with an understanding of the needs of the client, the development of services to meet those needs, pricing the services effectively, informing clients about the availability of the services, delivering them efficiently, and ensuring satisfaction during and after the exchange process. Following this six-step marketing process religiously and methodically should bring survival and growth in a dynamic and often turbulent marketplace.

What are the objectives of this book? The first objective is to educate the reader about what constitutes marketing. There is much confusion and misinformation about what marketing is or ought to be; this book will attempt to set the record straight. Second, a case will be built for why professional services providers need to market their services. Third, this book provides practical guidance to professionals who want to market their services in a thoughtful and progressive manner.

Who will benefit from this book? While the term "professional" has been bastardized quite badly over the past decade, there is a distinct and readily identifiable group of true professionals who are the intended audience. They share the commonalities of professional training, codes of ethics, and professional conduct. They include (but are not exclusive to) accountants, architects, attorneys, dentists, engineers, pharmacists, physicians, optometrists, and veterinarians. This book would also be a valuable addition to the material currently being used in courses given by trainers, instructors, or professors involved in services marketing.

This is my third book and every time I finish one I wonder whether or not it will structurally do the job. In this case I make a deliberate attempt to discuss concepts early in the book that will put everyone on an equal footing for the material that is presented later. The first chapter offers what I believe to be a succinct and realistic depiction of what marketing is or should be. Many readers will find this chapter a good review or a refresher while others will find it a novel or new perspective on marketing. Chapter Two offers a basic foundation for understanding professional services marketing and some basic propositions that any professional must accept if he or she truly wants to be marketing oriented. Failure to accept the basic premise found in Chapter Two may preclude the reader from embracing the marketing concept. Chapter Three offers a reasonable framework for the development of a marketing plan. Many of my professional services clients say they really appreciate this simple "cookbook" approach to marketing plan development. Chapter Four offers what I believe to be the essence of professional services marketing: client management. Client management is both a survival and a growth tool for professional services providers. If nothing else is gained from this book except an appreciation for the importance of this concept, then I will be happy. Chapter Five discusses the promotion of professional services and offers very practical advice for professionals who want to and must promote their services.

Many will find Chapter Six a little difficult to accept since it is not necessarily conventional thinking — marketing as a management tool? After reading it, however, I hope the reader will agree that it is a simple and adroitly obvious solution to the problems encountered when managing in a professional services environment. Chapter Seven offers a tangible and pragmatic approach to trade area and site analysis as well as physical facility evaluation. Chapter Eight focuses on one of the most critical aspects of professional services: communication. Unfortunately, research shows that many professionals have poor interpersonal and communication skills; this chapter provides some meaningful information on this topic and ways one can improve in this area. Chapter Nine provides an overview on what I believe the future holds for professional services marketing and how professionals can ensure that they will be able to survive and grow in the years ahead.

I think professional services providers will find this book enjoyable to read and I trust each and every one of them will find something of value within these pages. As a marketer I will not be satisfied unless my intended audience is satisfied. I truly hope this book will prompt them to action; to embrace the marketing philosophy as their way of doing business.

F. G. Crane, PhD

Chapter One

Understanding the Marketing Concept

DEFINING MARKETING

Most people, including professional services providers, have a narrow view of marketing. Yet, in a competitive environment, embracing the marketing concept may be the edge required not only to survive but to prosper. Why is marketing so important? First, it is the only business function that can generate revenue for an organization. More importantly, marketing is not just a business function, it is a philosophy, a state of mind, a way of doing business. Marketing puts the needs of the consumer ahead of the producer. In other words, what differentiates marketing from selling is the focus on consumer needs. Many professionals believe that when they complete their professional training a demand will exist for their services; after all, they are now qualified to deliver those services. If people do not know about the service or do not need the service, however, consumers will not beat a path to the door of the newly minted professional.

The American Marketing Association (1985) defines marketing as "the process of planning and executing the conception, pricing, promotion, and distribution of ideas, goods, and services to create exchanges that satisfy individual and organizational objectives." Two key words must be highlighted from this definition: exchange and satisfaction. Simply put, marketing is about exchange and achieving satisfaction during and after the exchange process.

In any exchange process, two people are required. In marketing this consists of buyer and seller. For satisfactory exchanges to occur, both parties must receive something of value; there must be equity in the exchange process. During and after the exchange process, both parties must be satisfied. If not, this will negate the prospects of continued and ongoing exchanges. For professional services marketers, as we will see, the concept of consumer satisfaction is central to long-term success.

THE PRODUCTION, SALES, AND MARKETING ERAS

The marketing concept is actually a relatively recent phenomenon. It has been argued that business has evolved from a production era, to a sales era, to the marketing era. Early in North American history, goods were scarce so buyers were willing to accept any goods that were produced. Essentially, production created its own demand. Emphasis was placed on production since the assumption was that products would sell themselves. By the 1920s, however, many businesses were producing more goods than buyers could consume. Competition increased and consumers had greater availability and choice of products. Business then entered the sales era. Salespeople were employed to find markets and consumers for products. This period lasted until 1960 for many organizations. Many are still in the sales era; they continue to produce what they produce best and hope to sell it.

The marketing era was and is characterized by a consumer orientation. Organizations embracing the marketing concept focused on satisfying the needs of consumers while simultaneously achieving organizational objectives. In the marketing era, selling is just one element of marketing. Also, instead of simply producing products and attempting to sell them, organizations actually consider what the market needs before production begins.

THE SIX KEY STEPS
IN THE MARKETING PROCESS

In the marketing era, marketing is viewed as a process and as a way of integrating a broad range of activities. The six key steps in the marketing process are seen in Figure 1-1.

FIGURE 1-1. The Six Steps in the Marketing Process

1. Identifying and comprehending consumer needs.
2. Developing products to meet those needs.
3. Pricing products effectively.
4. Informing consumers that the products exist.
5. Delivering the products efficiently.
6. Ensuring satisfaction during and after the exchange process.

The marketing concept holds that customer needs are central. Thus, marketing-oriented organizations start at step one of the process seen in Figure 1-1. Others, including professional services providers, often start at step two, or from a production orientation. Unfortunately, this is often a fatal mistake. Organizations using a production orientation find themselves falling into a subsequent sales orientation; they have produced a product and now must sell it. Some marketing theorists suggest that if an organization embraces a true marketing orientation, selling may be superfluous.

The marketing philosophy holds that the consumer is a seeker of solutions to his or her needs. The marketer then takes on the position of problem solver. Effective marketers offer appropriate solutions to the consumers' problems. Thus, proper identification and comprehension of consumers' needs is the appropriate starting point for effective marketing to occur.

THE MARKETING MIX

Marketers have a great deal of control over what products to offer the consumer, what price to charge, where to distribute the products, and how to inform the consumer of the products' availability. This is often referred to as the management of the marketing mix. The controllable marketing mix factors have been termed the Four P's by McCarthy (1964). Figure 1-2 depicts the Four P's or marketing mix.

FIGURE 1-2. The Marketing Mix—Four P's

Product: good or service designed to satisfy a consumer's needs

Price: what is exchanged for the product

Promotion: a way of informing the buyer about the product

Place: how to deliver (distribute) the product to the consumer

---

In Chapter Two we will see how the traditional Four P's have been expanded for professional services marketing to the Seven P's.

THE MARKETING ENVIRONMENT

Marketers do not operate in a vacuum. While marketers can exert a great deal of control over the development and execution of the marketing mix, there is an external environment that the marketer must consider and contend with on a continual basis. The factors that are beyond the control of the marketer are commonly referred to as environmental or uncontrollable factors. These factors can be placed into five broad categories as seen in Figure 1-3.

FIGURE 1-3. Five Broad Environmental Factors Affecting Marketing

1. Social/Demographic
2. Economic
3. Technological
4. Competitive
5. Legal/Regulatory

These environmental factors affect marketers and their decision-making processes. These factors can serve as opportunities or hurdles to the marketer, but either way they must always be considered when planning the marketing mix and a marketing program. In Chapter Three we will see the importance of a proper environmental scan when attempting to develop and execute a professional services marketing plan.

TARGET MARKETING VS. MASS MARKETING

The manipulation and synchronization of the elements of the marketing mix (the Four P's) is dependent on the market to be served. In general, a market is made up of people with the need and ability to buy a specific product. Since marketers cannot satisfy all consumers, they must select a specific group of consumers and direct their marketing effort toward them. When an organization selects a segment of the entire market to serve, this is the organization's target market. All too often organizations attempt to be all things to all people; they attempt a mass marketing approach. It is virtually impossible to be successful in business today with a mass marketing mentality.

Target marketing is a must in today's marketplace. Marketers must select the target market or segment of the market they feel they can best serve. This is where the matching process of marketing comes into play. Marketers must match the needs of the selected target market with an appropriate marketing mix.

MARKET SEGMENTATION

Through market segmentation a professional services firm can select a target market. This process involves dividing the mass market into submarkets or segments containing potential customers. The key to successful segmentation is to group together those consumers who have common needs and who will respond similarly to the marketing mix which will be executed. This is probably one of the most difficult tasks facing a marketer today. Many marketers do not segment the market enough and fail to see the differences between groups of potential customers. On the other hand, there is also the possibility of oversegmenting. Taken to its extreme, segmenting too much can be just as bad as mass marketing. For any market segment to be operationalized it must meet four basic criteria. Figure 1-4 shows the four specific criteria for segmentation.

FIGURE 1-4. Criteria for Market Segmentation

1. Similarity of potential buyers' needs within a segment
2. Differences in needs of buyers between segments
3. Potential for profitability
4. Ability to reach the segment

Market segmentation should be seen as only a means to an end. It is carried out to allow a firm to design an appropriate marketing mix and marketing program that will satisfy the target market's needs. There are a number of variables that can be used to segment a market. Generally, those variables can be grouped into two broad categories:

1. Customer Characteristics—including geographics (where customers live), demographics (age, gender, income, family size) and psychographics (personality and lifestyle).
2. Buying Situations—including benefits sought by consumers and usage rates.

Often marketers focus on demographics as a segmentation variable. While demographics is a useful starting point to profile potential segments, it usually tells us the least about the consumers' buying behavior. Demographics will tell us who is buying and what they buy but certainly will not tell us why. Thus marketers must try to use several segmentation variables to profile a target market. Essentially, a combination of segmentation variables should answer the following questions:

1. Who buys and where?
2. How do they buy?
3. How much do they buy?
4. Why do they buy?

If market segmentation and target market profiling is done correctly, answers to the above questions should be provided. Professional service firms often fail to recognize that there are differences between potential consumers in the market. This creates a problem in adequately designing a marketing mix and marketing program to appeal to a target market. Figure 1-5 illustrates how a professional services client may be profiled using several segmentation variables.

FIGURE 1-5. Profile of a Possible Professional Services Client

Geographics:	City Center — Metropolitan Boston
Demographics:	Male, 35-44 years of age, single or married, no children, earning $50,000 or more, college graduate
Psychographics:	Aggressive, extroverted, values time, heavy magazine and newspaper readership
Benefits Sought:	Seeks high quality, personal service; not price-sensitive
Usage Rate:	Moderate to heavy user

Segmentation is an integral part of the marketing process. By segmenting markets effectively, marketers can assess the extent of marketing opportunities that may exist in given markets. It also enables the marketer to tailor the product offering with precision given the nature of the market segment. Finally, segmentation also allows for an effective and efficient marketing program to be developed.

SUMMARY

1. Professional services providers must embrace marketing in order to be successful in today's marketplace.

2. Central to the marketing concept are the needs of the client. Marketing is about equitable exchange and client satisfaction.

3. The six steps in the marketing process are: (1) identifying and comprehending consumers' needs; (2) developing products (services) to meet their needs; (3) pricing products effectively; (4) informing consumers about the products; (5) delivering the

products efficiently; and (6) ensuring client satisfaction during and after the exchange process.

4. The marketing mix (Four P's) or factors controlled by the marketer. They include product, price, promotion, and place (distribution).

5. The uncontrollable or environmental factors that influence marketing activities include: (1) social/demographic factors; (2) economic factors; (3) technological factors; (4) competitive factors; and (5) legal/regulatory factors.

6. Target marketing is a must for professional services providers. A target market, or segment of the entire market, must be selected to be served by the professional services marketer.

7. Any market segment must meet four criteria: (1) potential buyers within the segment need to be similar; (2) potential buyers within the segment must be different from other segments; (3) the segment must be profitable; and (4) the marketer must be able to reach the segment.

8. Variables used to segment a market include: (1) customer characteristics (e.g., geographics, demographics, and psychographics) and (2) buying situations (e.g., benefits sought by the consumer and usage rates).

9. It is critical that segmentation variables answer the following questions about clients in a segment: (1) who buys and where? (2) how do they buy? (3) how much do they buy? and (4) why do they buy?

10. Professional services providers need to design an appropriate marketing mix and marketing program to reach a well-defined target market or segment.

REFERENCES

"AMA Board Approves New Marketing Definition," *Marketing News*, March 1, 1985, p. 1.

McCarthy, E. Jerome. *Basic Marketing*, 2nd Ed., Homewood: Irwin, 1964.

Chapter Two

Professional Services Marketing

DEFINING PROFESSIONAL SERVICES

There is no generally accepted definition of what constitutes a professional or a professional service. In fact, the word professional is often so bastardized in the marketplace it is difficult to find any occupation that has not added the term *professional* to their title. However, there is one excellent definition proposed by Gummesson. The definition states:

> A professional service is qualified, it is advisory and problem-solving, even though it may encompass some routine work for clients. The professionals involved have a common identity, like physicians, lawyers, accountants or engineers, and are regulated by traditions and codes of ethics. The service offered, if accepted, involves the professional in taking on assignments for the client and those assignments are themselves the limit of the professional's involvement. Such assignments are not undertaken to merely sell hardware or other services. (1981, p. 108)

The key operational concepts of this definition are the problem-solving and advisory roles that must be played by professional services marketers. Many marketers believe that the marketing of services may be completely different from the marketing of goods. However, marketing as a process and as a functional area of business can be applied to both.

The same six-step process discussed in Chapter One can be applied to marketing professional services. But a different approach or shift in emphasis in marketing management and strategy is required for professional services. Professional services marketing is different than goods marketing for two reasons. First, there are generic differences between goods and professional services. Second, there is a difference in the management environment or context within which marketing tasks must be planned and executed in the professional services arena. Professional services, then, is a unique product that has to be understood, managed, and marketed differently from a packaged good.

CHARACTERISTICS OF PROFESSIONAL SERVICES

The key characteristics of professional services which are the main source of difficulty in managing and marketing professional services are seen in Figure 2-1. These characteristics have been referred to as the Four I's (Berkowitz et al., 1991). We will discuss each of these elements of professional services in some detail.

FIGURE 2-1. The Four I's of Professional Services

1. Intangibility
2. Inventory
3. Inconsistency
4. Inseparability

Intangibility

One of the basic and most cited characteristics of professional services is intangibility. Intangibility pertains to the inability of professional services to be seen, felt, tasted, or touched in the same manner in which goods can be sensed. For the most part, professional services cannot be displayed, physically demonstrated or illustrated. The concept of intangibility presents a challenge to professional services marketers. The professional services marketer must tell a consumer what the service will do and this may have to be accomplished without the benefit of illustration, demonstration, or display. This creates difficulty in promoting a professional service. Often professional services marketers are forced to use tangible surrogates as a means to promote an intangible product. In other words, because of intangibility, professional services marketers need to make their services more tangible and to show benefits of using their service. In Chapter Four we will discuss how this can be accomplished through the use of impression management.

Inventory

The ability to inventory professional services capacity is virtually impossible. Professional services are perishable and demand for professional services tends to fluctuate by season, by week or even by day, or time of day. Unused capacity to serve cannot be stored and saved. Service storage inability and demand fluctuations create many problems for professional services marketers.

Often professional services marketers find it difficult to handle peak load demands (too much demand and too little capacity to serve), while at other times service facilities remain idle. Often consumer satisfaction with professional services marketers is influenced by whether or not the service firm can cope with demand. On the other hand, idle capacity is a problem for professional services marketers. If a physician is paid to see patients but no one schedules an appointment, the fixed cost of the idle physician's salary is a high inventory carrying cost. The concept of synchronizing supply and demand is important for professional services marketers. We will see in Chapter Four how synchromarketing can be used in professional services marketing.

Inconsistency

Professional services marketing is also challenging because the quality of service is often inconsistent. Because professional services depend on the people who provide them, the quality of service may vary because people have different capabilities.

Additionally, while inconsistency can occur across individuals, variance in service quality can also occur in the day-to-day job performances of the same individual. Performance can also depend on level of demand; in periods of high demand, a professional service provider may not spend as much time or exert as much effort as in periods of low demand.

This variability is often problematic for professional services marketers. Consumers cannot be certain about the performance of the professional services provider on a given day, even if they use the same service provider on a regular basis. The reduction of inconsistency can be tied to a comprehensive client management program (see Chapter Four).

Inseparability

While tangible goods are produced, sold, and then consumed, professional services are sold, then produced and consumed simultaneously. Because of inseparability, the consumer must be present in the service system to receive the service. The consumer is also an active participant in producing the professional service and thereby can affect the performance and quality of the professional service delivered. For example, a physician's diagnosis or an accountant's tax advice requires both the presence and the active participation of the consumer. The accuracy and effectiveness of the professional will often depend on the consumer's specifications, communications, and degree of participation in the production of the professional service.

In other words, how well the professional services provider performs depends on how well the consumer performs. Because of inseparability the professional services marketer needs to offer the service at the right place and at the right time for the consumer. How effectively the professional and consumer interact and participate together in creating and delivering the service, however, will be the key to determining whether or not future exchanges will occur. This will be discussed further in Chapter Four.

THE MARKETING MIX
FOR PROFESSIONAL SERVICES —
THE SEVEN P's

Chapter One introduced you to the Four P's or the marketing mix. This original list of the marketing mix elements needs to be adapted and expanded in order to take into consideration the uniqueness of professional services. Booms and Bitner (1981) offer a modification and expansion to the existing marketing mix framework that is more appropriate for professional services marketers. Figure 2-2 depicts the Seven P's (Marketing Mix) for professional services marketing. We will discuss the three additional P's added to the original marketing mix, namely people, physical evidence, and process.

FIGURE 2-2. The Seven P's (Marketing Mix)
for Professional Services

1. Product
2. Price
3. Promotion
4. Place
5. People
6. Physical Evidence
7. Process

People

This includes all people who play a part in the professional service delivery process and who can influence the consumer's perception of the service. It consists of the personnel in the professional services firm as well as other consumers in the services environment. The personnel who perform a role in the service production or delivery process may be perceived by the consumer as part of the service. These personnel may play a dual role of performing the service and marketing the service. The critical role of personnel in service production and delivery means that employee recruitment, selection, training, and motivation become part of the marketing activity of the professional services firm. Success in professional services marketing is partly contingent on recognizing the importance of consumer contact personnel (see Chapter Four).

In addition to contact personnel, consumers can be influenced by noncontact personnel and other consumers who are present in the service system. The problem for professional services marketers is controlling how noncontact personnel can support contact personnel as well as regulating the composition of consumers and the nature of the interactions between consumers in the services environment.

Physical Evidence

Physical evidence includes the physical environment where the service is provided and all tangible clues that a consumer can examine in order to derive an impression of the professional service. This is discussed in detail in Chapter Four (Impression Management).

Process

This involves the actual procedures, mechanisms, and flow of activities by which the professional service is delivered. Consumers of professional services are not only interested in what they receive in the end from the professional services provider, they are also interested in how they receive the professional service. The concepts of technical and functional quality of the service process are discussed in Chapter Four.

PREFACE FOR PROFESSIONAL SERVICES MARKETING

Before the anatomy of a professional services marketing plan can be discussed (Chapter Three), the professional must be prepared to embrace marketing as a philosophy and as a way of doing business. What follows is a series of propositions designed to enhance critical thinking about the scope and nature of professional services marketing. They provide a foundation and understanding of why the professional should be marketing oriented as well as construct a professional services marketing plan.

Proposition 1 – Professional services marketers need to market their services.

Professional services marketers cannot continue to believe that their services will market themselves. Professionals can no longer expect to hang a shingle and find consumers beating a path to their door. Competition has increased and consumers have become more sophisticated. Obtaining clients by chance can no longer work. Profitability is not a dirty word and in order to survive and to prosper, the professional services provider needs to accept marketing as part of his or her practice philosophy.

Proposition 2 – Professionals need to be marketers.

In addition to the need to market professional services, the professional services provider needs to be a marketer. It is not incongruent to be a professional and at the same time to build and expand a professional services business. Since marketing is about satisfying needs of clients, professionals must by definition be marketers. Professionals must satisfy the needs of existing clients but must also actively market their services to new and prospective clients. Even professional services firms that are large enough to hire marketing expertise should not delegate the marketing process or reject responsibility for practice development. Everyone in a professional service firm is a marketer. All must work together to provide a service that satisfies the client.

Proposition 3 – The client's needs should always take precedence over the professional's needs.

This is probably one of the most difficult propositions for professionals to accept. But remember that marketing is the science of exchange; both parties must receive equity in the exchange process. The professional only obtains profitability as a result of offering a satisfactory service to the client. In other words, the client needs to receive what he or she desires before the service provider receives what he or she desires. While a professional may have the technical ability to supply a service, it must be the right one for the client. Developing and marketing the proper service come as a result of a client needs assessment.

Proposition 4 – Professional services marketing requires time and money.

Marketing must be seen as a systematic, comprehensive, and ongoing process. As such, marketing requires an investment. Professional services marketers must set aside both time and money for marketing activities. This means both a short-term and a long-term commitment.

Proposition 5 – Professional services marketing means being opportunistic.

Professional services marketers need to be open and receptive to new opportunities. Every day, the professional must discover and seize opportunities to market existing services better, to develop new services, and to maintain a competitive edge.

Professionals have always done some marketing yet its application has usually been fragmented. Often marketing has been conducted under the guise of public relations. Today's marketplace requires that professionals apply marketing in the same professional manner as they carry out their professional duties.

SUMMARY

1. A professional service involves offering qualified, advisory, and problem-solving skills to clients.

2. The characteristics that make professional services marketing and management difficult are the Four I's: (1) intangibility; (2) inventory; (3) inconsistency; and (4) inseparability.

3. Intangibility makes it difficult for the professional services

provider to demonstrate the service. Often tangible surrogates are needed to promote the intangible service.

4. Professionals cannot store their capacity (inventory) to serve. Many times a professional has idle capacity while at other times has too little capacity to serve.

5. Because professional services depend on people to deliver them, the quality of service often varies across service providers or even the day-to-day performance of the same service provider (inconsistency).

6. The client must be present in the service system to receive the service (inseparability). This required active participation by the client can influence the quality of the professional service.

7. The Seven P's of the professional services marketing mix include: (1) product; (2) price; (3) promotion; (4) place; (5) people; (6) physical evidence; and (7) process.

8. The people involved, the physical evidence surrounding the service, and the process of producing and delivering professional services are critically important for the professional services provider to manage.

9. Professional services providers need to market their services and be active marketers themselves. Professionals must be prepared to devote time and money to the marketing function and to be opportunistic at all times.

10. Professionals need to be as committed to marketing as they are to their professional duties.

REFERENCES

Berkowitz, Eric N., Roger A. Kerin, William Rudelius and Frederick G. Crane. *Marketing*, 1st Canadian Ed., Homewood: Irwin, 1991.

Booms, Bernard H. and Mary J. Bitner. "Marketing Strategies and Organization Structures for Service Firms," in *Marketing Services*, James H. Donnelly and William R. George (eds.), Chicago: American Marketing Association, 1981, pp. 47-51.

Gummesson, Evert. "The Marketing of Professional Services," in *Marketing Services*, James H. Donnelly and William R. George (eds.), Chicago: American Marketing Association, 1981, pp. 108-112.

Chapter Three

The Anatomy of a Professional Services Marketing Plan

WHY A MARKETING PLAN?

To be successful in the professional services market, a firm must have three basic ingredients:

1. A service that is oriented to client needs.
2. An organizational structure and culture that is effective in delivering the service.
3. A marketing plan that identifies strategies and responsibilities for implementing a marketing program designed to achieve realistic objectives.

All three ingredients are equally important. To be weak in any often spells failure. A weak organizational structure and culture or inadequate planning can ruin the best professional service and creative planning cannot compensate for a poor professional service. However, a skillfully devised marketing plan can strengthen both the service and the organization. The marketing plan should be thought of as a road map or a guide to growth and success. But a plan must not only be created, it should also be put to work. Planning and execution must come together in a mutually reinforcing way.

This chapter offers a suggested approach for developing a marketing plan. When developing a marketing plan, a professional services firm should ask three basic questions:

1. Where are we now?
2. Where are we going?
3. How we are going to get there?

To answer the first two questions, the professional services firm needs to conduct an internal marketing audit as well as an environmental scan. Once they are complete, a SWOT analysis (internal Strengths, Weaknesses, and external Opportunities and Threats) can be completed. Next, a firm can set its objectives (where it can and wants to go). The marketing plan can then be completed which addresses the third question, how we are going to get there? The marketing plan logically flows from the audit, scan, and SWOT analysis. The marketing plan itself should be the road map or the blueprint for practice development. Figure 3-1 shows the basic anatomy of a professional services marketing plan. In this chapter we shall cover in some detail all those basic elements that are an integral part of the plan.

FIGURE 3-1. Anatomy of a Professional Services Marketing Plan

1. Internal Marketing Audit
2. Environmental Scan
3. SWOT Analysis
4. Marketing Objectives
5. Marketing Strategy and Competitive Advantage
6. Marketing Program
7. Sales/Profit Forecasts and Marketing Budget
8. Control and Evaluation Measures

THE INTERNAL MARKETING AUDIT

When one hears the word audit, financial auditing usually comes to mind. However, there is such a thing as a marketing audit. Whereas the financial audit examines the health of a firm from a financial perspective, a marketing audit examines it from a marketing perspective. A marketing audit can be defined as:

> A comprehensive, systematic examination of a firm's total marketing activities. It examines all the marketing controllable factors (or the marketing mix) on a diagnosis and prognosis basis. The marketing audit should always be conducted in conjunction with the environmental scan and before the marketing plan is constructed.

The audit should be as objective as possible and often professional services firms find it necessary to seek the outside objective advice of a marketing firm. The audit should determine internal strengths and weaknesses and provide the firm with an indication of where it is as well as where it is going.

Figure 3-2 shows the principal components of a professional services audit.

FIGURE 3-2. Components of a Professional Services Audit

1. Practice philosophy
2. Physical operating environment
3. Client base
4. Service process and delivery
5. Professional fees
6. Communications

Hard questions are necessary, as is hard evidence to support the answers. Figure 3-3 shows the type of questions that should be part of the internal marketing audit.

FIGURE 3-3. Marketing Audit Questions

Practice Philosophy

1. What is the current practice philosophy?
2. What is the mission of the firm?
3. Who is responsible for the development of philosophy and mission?
4. What is the basic service concept being offered to our clients?

Physical Operating Environment

1. What is the current level of marketing practice and activities?
2. What factors inhibit or assist the adoption of a marketing orientation?
3. Does a written marketing plan exist?
4. Are there any changes in the operating levels of the firm?

Client Base

1. Who are the main users of the firm's services?
2. How can the clients be classified or segmented?
3. Which clients are profitable?
4. What is the client's frequency and quantity of use?
5. What is the attrition rate? Why is it occurring?

Service Process and Delivery

1. Is the firm successful in completing work on time?
2. Is there a quality control process?
3. What procedures are in place to ensure effective delivery of service?
4. Is the level of client service adequate?
5. How are service quality and reliability viewed by clients?

Professional Fees

1. Are the fees charges consistent with image and reputation?
2. How do fees compare to competitors' fees?
3. Are clients satisfied or dissatisfied with fees charged?
4. Are fees set to produce volume or profit?
5. Is there costing information for each type of service offered?

Communications

1. What is the nature and quality of inhouse communications?
2. What is the nature and quality of external communications?
3. Does the firm have a standardized client consultation procedure?
4. How are the interpersonal skills of the staff?
5. What is the state of the visual identity of the firm?
6. Is the correct message and medium being used for external communications?

THE ENVIRONMENTAL SCAN

In addition to conducting an internal marketing audit, a professional services firm should carry out an external environmental scan. Professional services marketers should continually acquire and assess information on events that occur outside the firm. The purpose of the scan is to identify and interpret potential trends and their impact on the professional services firm. Through environmental scanning the professional services marketer can determine whether or not trends in the market environment pose specific opportunities or threats. It should be noted that an environmental trend that represents an important opportunity for one professional service firm may be a major threat to another and vice versa.

The broad environmental and uncontrollable factors described in Figure 1-3 in Chapter One should form the basis of an environmental scan. Figure 3-4 shows key trends that may be important for professional services marketers in the 1990s. Each professional services firm should evaluate both national and regional trends and determine which trends are most important when developing a marketing plan. The results from an environmental scan must be measured and weighed against the results of the internal marketing audit.

SWOT ANALYSIS

Taken together the audit and the scan can form a SWOT analysis (internal strengths and weaknesses and external opportunities and threats). The objective of a SWOT analysis is to help a firm comprehensively view the factors that must be considered when selecting the proper marketing strategy and developing a marketing program. Figure 3-5 shows an example of how a SWOT analysis can be constructed.

FIGURE 3-4. An Example of an Environmental Scan

Environmental Factor	Trend Identified
Social/Demographic	Increased aging; the rise of the grey market
	Population shifting to urban areas
	Increase demand for quality and service
	Greater role of women in economy
Economic	Decline in real income for many consumers
	Greater consumer acceptance of debt
	Rising concern over inflation/recession
Technological	Increased use of computerization
	Advances in communications
	Greater use of robotics
	Growth in biotechnology
Competitive	Lower entry barriers to professions
	Increase in small, innovative firms
	Downsizing, restructuring of large firms
	Increased international competition
	Aggressive promotional activities
Legal/Regulatory	Greater concern over ethics in business
	Decreased regulation over promotion
	Greater concern over practice liability
	Growth in self-regulation
	Increased consumerism

Every professional services marketer wishing to develop a marketing plan would be well advised to conduct a marketing audit and an environmental scan and to construct a SWOT analysis. This type of analysis will provide valuable input into the strategy selection and marketing plan development phase.

FIGURE 3-5. An Example of a SWOT Analysis

Able Accountants

	Strengths	**Weaknesses**
Internal	Quality service Respected image Financial stability Locational convenience	No clear strategic direction High overhead High staff turnover High level of receivables
	Opportunities	**Threats**
External	High-tech innovations Less regulation Joint venturing	Saturation of markets Strong price competition Recessionary economy

MARKETING OBJECTIVES

Once the audit and environmental scan (plus SWOT analysis) is complete, a firm can set its objectives (where it can and wants to go). A professional services firm must develop the specific objectives it seeks to achieve and by which it can measure its performance. A professional services firm must earn a profit to survive. Profit is considered a dirty word by many. However, profit is the reward the professional services marketer receives for the risk taken when offering the service to a client.

Many professional services marketers believe one of their primary objectives is to serve the public good while maintaining a reasonable level of profit. Social responsibility can and should be an integral part of a professional services marketer's objectives. This may even be accomplished at the expense of some profitability. But a professional services firm needs to maintain some level of profit in order to survive. Marketing objectives must meet five specifications in order to be considered good objectives. Figure 3-6 shows the five specifications marketing objectives must meet.

FIGURE 3-6. Five Specifications for Marketing Objectives

1. An objective should relate to a single, specific topic (e.g., one for profit level, one for market share, etc.).
2. An objective should relate to a result not to an activity to be performed.
3. An objective should be measurable (quantitative if possible).
4. An objective should contain a time deadline for its achievement.
5. An objective should be challenging but achievable.

In essence, good marketing objectives should involve precise statements of results sought, quantified in time and magnitude if possible, and they should be realistic. Arriving at reasonable objectives requires involvement from all members of the professional services organization. There should be a sense of ownership in the objectives. Tying personal objectives and the firm's objectives together will create greater synergy of effort and will benefit both the employees and the firm.

UNDERSTANDING MARKETING STRATEGY

The strategic marketing process involves efforts by an organization to identify and select market opportunities, to allocate resources, and to develop marketing plans to capitalize on selected opportunities. Two key factors characterize a marketing strategy: (1) a specified target market and (2) a marketing program to reach it. Although the term marketing strategy is often used loosely, it implies both the end sought (target market) and the means to achieve it (marketing program). The marketing strategy is the means by which objectives are to be achieved. Two important concepts in marketing strategy are competitive advantage and growth options.

The Concept of Competitive Advantage

Marketers search continuously to find a sustainable competitive advantage, a strength relative to their competitors likely to be maintained in the market they serve or the product they offer. Generally, marketing research suggests that two broad general strategies are available in order to be successful in today's marketplace: (1) superiority based on performance (e.g., better product [service], better distribution, or better promotion) or (2) superiority in terms of price (low cost).

A professional service firm can attempt to offer a better service or a better price, but generally not both. Many professional services firms shy away from competing on a price dimension. This is because consumers often use price as a surrogate indicator of quality. A very low price in professional services marketing may be viewed negatively by the consumer as opposed to a positive way to differentiate a service.

So, superiority in terms of product (service) offered often becomes the focus for the professional services organization. However, an organization can also consider differentiation or superiority in terms of place (distribution) or promotion. In fact, many experts believe that many professional services firms have the ability to offer comparable services. As such, differentiation may only occur through better distribution (e.g., locational convenience) or by creating a perception of differentiation through promotion. Differences in professional services today may more likely be achieved through image or psychological differentiation. This concept of achieving differentiation through promotion is discussed in Chapter Five.

Strategic Options for Growth

Many marketers discuss strategic growth options and the concept of competitive advantage separately thus creating the illusion that decisions regarding growth options and competitive advantage are linear or sequential. In fact, growth option selection and competitive advantage are integrally linked. The professional services marketer looking to obtain revenue or expand revenue must consider how this can be achieved. Sometimes a professional services marketer considers what the competitive advantage is and, at the same time, determines the best market in which to apply that competitive advantage. Others determine the growth option and then consider what competitive advantage will be needed to accomplish it.

In general, a firm that wants to achieve growth and profitability can attempt to (1) increase revenues, (2) decrease expenses, or (3) do both. We will focus on options designed to generate or increase revenue. There are a number of strategic options available to the professional services marketer in order to do so. We will discuss the interrelationship between competitive advantage and strategic growth options in some detail. Figure 3-7 shows the growth options available to the professional services organization.

FIGURE 3-7. Strategic Growth Options

1. Market penetration
2. Market development
3. Product development
4. Diversification

Market Penetration

Market penetration involves attempting to expand market share and sales of existing products in an existing market. This can be accomplished through superior product (service), competitive pricing (superior price), or through better distribution or aggressive promotion. The increase in market share can occur through increasing the usage rates of existing clients, or by attracting nonusers or competitors' clients. Market penetration is generally the easiest and least risky option for professionals to pursue, at least initially. However, once a market becomes mature and saturated, other strategic growth options may have to be selected to maintain growth.

Market Development

This involves taking an existing product into a new market. For professional services this normally involves geographic expansion or multisite development. Generally, the professional services firm would seek out a similar target segment in the new geographic market.

However, it could involve appealing to new market segments (develop a new target segment, or multisegment development). In most service businesses it is easier to achieve geographic expansion by simply taking the existing service to a new region and focusing on a similar target. Attempting to serve a different target segment in the existing market rather than a new geographic market may cause some difficulties. In trying to expand this way the professional services firm may alienate the existing target segment. The existing target may wonder why you are catering to a new segment and if your service is changing. On the other hand, the newly targeted segment may not respond to your marketing effort since their image of you is derived from the target you currently serve. Often different versions of the same service are used to appeal to the new segment. For example, say a new lower-priced version of your service is introduced to attract a new price-sensitive segment. This sends a new message and possibly a new image to existing clients which can cause conflict. Changing the existing service or using a new image to attract a new segment may be more risky than simply moving geographically via multisite development to service more clients similar to the existing segment. This option, in my opinion, is the one that should be considered after the market penetration option has been exhausted.

Product Development

This involves the development of a new or modified product to appeal to present markets. It emphasizes new service versions, quality improvements, line extensions, or other minor innovations closely related to established services and the marketing of such to existing clients.

Often service improvements are required to maintain a competitive advantage in an existing market. Such innovation can be designed to preempt competitive entry. Developing new products (services) is risky and should probably be considered after market penetration and market development options have been exhausted.

Diversification

This involves the professional services firm offering new products aimed at new markets. Generally this option involves expansion into unrelated lines of business. It is often utilized to avoid over-dependency on the existing business. This is the option with the most risk and should be considered with caution.

In order to understand how growth options can be selected and how competitive advantage fits into the process, consider that a medical practice specializing in women's wellness clinics in Boston was begun ten years ago. The product offered was superior (competitive advantage) and it was offered to a unique market segment. The product had been developed (product development) and had penetrated the Boston market (market penetration). Because of its success the service attracted competitors to its market. Much of the competition had been defended against or warded off (defending market share) by providing excellent service and by aggressive promotion. Even so, the practice found it difficult to achieve further growth through greater penetration.

In an effort to improve the situation the concept was taken to a new market (market development) by physically expanding about five years ago into Maine, where there was little competition. This expansion was also driven by nonmarketing factors (e.g., the service provider's family wanted to live there). Competitive advantage allowed this market to be penetrated. Two years ago, it was determined that further market penetration in either the Boston or Maine markets was not possible with the existing service. It was therefore decided to expand the service offering to the present market. It was discovered that a large number of existing clients, especially seniors, had difficulty getting to the clinics. An old-fashioned house-call service was developed (product development). The house-call service was available twenty-four hours a day, seven days a week. The younger associates currently working in the clinics could handle the bulk of the demand and a few new associates were hired on a part-time basis to handle excess demand.

The Boston and Maine markets have been successfully penetrated with the wellness clinics and the newly developed product, the house-call service, also has penetrated the market. Currently, new options are being considered. It is believed that all opportunities in medicine that are available or of interest have been exhausted.

The practice is now considering diversification, a new line of business unrelated to medicine. A friend convinces the professional to invest in a land development project in Maine. The objective is to develop an upscale resort near the ocean in Maine. It will cater to the upscale business convention market and the luxury-seeking individual traveller. The competitive advantage will be a premium product bundled with outstanding service.

This example illustrates the usual and often the most logical path to selecting growth options. We moved from market penetration to market development, to product development and then to diversification. Growth options may not be selected in the manner shown, but the progression illustrated usually involves the least risk. It is also possible to use and combine two or more growth options at the same time. Also, it should be noted that there is spillover across the alternatives. For example, in order to use market penetration the service must first be developed (product development), or the service firm can be penetrating an existing market while at the same time developing a new market geographically.

THE MARKETING PROGRAM

We saw earlier that a marketing strategy involves a specified target market and a marketing program to reach that target market. While strategy provides the basic road map, a marketing program involves the detailed day-to-day operational decisions essential to the overall success of the marketing strategy. To implement strategy many decisions are often required, such as determining promotional budgets or making pricing decisions. These decisions are tactical and involve actions that must be taken immediately or in the short term in order to effectively execute strategy. The marketing program lays out how the marketing mix variables (Seven P's) will be manipulated and leveraged.

The marketing program spells out how each of the marketing mix elements will be operationalized. The major component of the professional services marketing plan will involve details on the marketing program. Under the marketing program section of the marketing plan, specific statements about product (service) price, place promotion, people, physical evidence, and process must be made. Precision and detail are required here. Each of the marketing mix elements must be synchronized. Decisions about one aspect of the marketing mix must be considered in light of the other elements.

The marketing program should cover the Seven P's in some detail. The following list illustrates some of the decision areas that must be considered under the marketing program component of the marketing plan.

1. *Product (service).* What will be the range of services offered? What will be the level of quality? Will product (service) be used as a competitive advantage or differentiator? Will there be guarantees? What will be the after-the-sale service level?

2. *Price.* What will be the pricing or fee levels? Will there be discounts for some clients? What will be the payment terms? Will credit be offered? Will price be used to differentiate service?

3. *Place.* What will be the location for the service? How accessible will the location be? Will others be used to distribute the service? Will place be used to differentiate the service?

4. *Promotion.* What will be the promotional mix? How much money will be spent on promotion? How will promotional efforts be evaluated? Will promotion be used to differentiate the service?

5. *People.* What types of people will be hired? What kind of training will they receive? What role will they play in service provision? How will they be compensated? Will our people be used to differentiate the service?

6. *Physical Evidence.* What will the service environment look like? What cues should be managed and controlled? Will physical evidence be used to differentiate the service?
7. *Process.* What will be the practice policies? What will be the basic procedures for developing and delivering the service? What role will computers and automation play in the process? What role will the client play in the process? What will be the quality control measures? Will the delivery process be used to differentiate the service?

EFFECTIVELY IMPLEMENTING MARKETING PROGRAMS

There is no formula for effective implementation of the marketing program. However, there are some basic guidelines that can assist you in effectively implementing a marketing program.

1. Communicate the content of the marketing program to the organization. Be certain that everyone understands what the objectives are and how they will be achieved.
2. Have someone responsible for the implementation. While everyone is ultimately part of the process and responsible for execution, one key person should be responsible for ensuring successful execution of the program.
3. Foster open communication. To ensure successful implementation of the program, foster a work environment that is open and honest so that any problems that arise can be discussed and solved.
4. Have precise tasks, responsibilities, and deadlines as part of the program. Successful implementation requires that people know the tasks for which they are responsible and are given deadlines for completing them. (The use of *action item lists* is a good idea. Action lists describe the task, the name of the people responsible for completing the task, and the date by which it is to be finished.)

5. Have a bias for action. Sometimes fine-tuning of the marketing program will be required but do not delay the program by overanalyzing it. Strive for about 90 percent perfection and let the marketplace help to fine-tune any elements that may require it.

MARKETING PLANNING VS. EXECUTION

Sometimes we hear the statement, "We had a good plan, but we didn't execute it." When a marketing program fails it is often difficult to determine whether it was a result of poor strategy or poor implementation. Sometimes a professional services firm will have the right strategy and effectively execute (good strategy, good execution). This will lead to success. Some will have a bad strategy but execute well (bad strategy, good execution). This case spells trouble unless the strategy can be corrected. Sometimes the strategy is correct but implementation has been ineffective (good strategy, bad execution). Again, this spells trouble and the implementation problem must be rectified. Finally and unfortunately, some professional services firms will have both the wrong strategy and also fail to execute well (bad strategy, bad execution).

For many years, marketers overemphasized execution rather than strategic planning. Now, many marketers are planning more, but unfortunately are executing less. A balance is required to be successful today. If anything, emphasis may often have to be placed on implementation since strategy without execution is useless.

SALES/PROFIT FORECASTS AND MARKETING BUDGET

The marketing plan will be designed to achieve certain objectives. Often sales and profit are part of the stated objectives.

Thus, part of the marketing plan should spell out sales and profit levels that will be expected as a result of the marketing program. Additionally, the marketing program is going to cost money to develop and execute. Estimates for how much the marketing effort will cost must be part of the written marketing plan. Decide on the specific marketing tasks to be undertaken and allocate the monies to carry them out.

CONTROL AND EVALUATION MEASURES

The marketing program must be closely monitored and evaluated. The essence of control, the final component of the marketing plan, is designed to compare results with planned objectives and to take any necessary actions required because of deviations from planned objectives.

Generally, management by exception is recommended here. That is, identify results that deviate from plans, diagnose their causes, and take new actions. If objectives were established correctly (quantitative and measurable), a benchmark exists to compare actual results. Part of the evaluation process will involve sales analysis, profitability analysis, and cost analysis.

AN EFFECTIVE MARKETING PLAN

Effective marketing plans should answer the following questions:

1. Where are we now and how did we get there?
2. Where are we going?
3. What is the best way to get there?
4. What actions are required to get there, by whom, and when?
5. What is it going to cost and what will be the return on investment?

6. What will be measured in order to control and evaluate the plan?

Effective marketing plans are often a result of managerial judgment and plenty of common sense. In addition to the plan addressing the six questions posed above, an effective marketing plan for professional services should:

1. Be based on sound facts and valid assumptions
2. Have specific marketing objectives
3. Have a sound strategy
4. Contain a simple, clear, and specific marketing program
5. Be self-contained and complete
6. Possess control and evaluation measures

SUMMARY

1. The marketing plan for a professional services provider should be viewed as a road map or guide to growth and success.

2. A marketing audit should be part of the plan. It examines the health of the firm from a marketing perspective.

3. An environmental scan is also a part of the marketing plan. The scan identifies trends in the environment that may impact on the firm.

4. Taken together, the audit and scan form a SWOT analysis, or the internal strengths and weaknesses and external opportunities and threats confronting the firm.

5. A professional services firm can then formulate marketing objectives. These objectives must be realistic, achievable, measurable, and contain a time deadline for achievement.

6. Two key factors characterize a marketing strategy: (1) a specific target market and (2) a marketing program to reach this market. The marketing strategy is the means by which objectives are to be achieved.

7. A competitive advantage is a strength relative to competi-

tors which is likely to be maintained in the market served or the product (service) offered. It usually involves superiority based on performance (product [service], distribution, or promotion) or superiority price.

8. There are four strategic growth options available to the professional services marketer: (1) market penetration, (2) market development, (3) product development, and (4) diversification. These options must be considered in concert with the concept of competitive advantage.

9. A marketing program involves the detailed day-to-day operational decisions essential to the successful execution of the selected marketing strategy. Tactical decisions regarding the Seven P's are made as part of the marketing program.

10. Effective implementation of the marketing program requires that (1) the content be communicated to the organization, (2) someone is responsible for implementation, (3) there is open communication, (4) precise tasks, responsibilities, and deadlines are part of the program, and (5) the program has a bias for action.

11. A balance between strategic planning and execution is required for effective marketing.

12. A marketing plan should also contain sales/profit and a marketing budget.

13. Finally, a good marketing plan will have control and evaluation measures. This usually includes sales, profitability, and cost analysis.

14. An effective marketing plan should answer these questions: (1) Where is the service now and how did it get there? (2) Where is it going? (3) What is the best way to get there? (4) What actions are required to get there, by whom, and when? (5) What is it going to cost and what will be the return on investment? and (6) What will be measured to control and evaluate the plan?

Chapter Four

Client Management — A Critical Tool

In the search for a sustainable competitive advantage, professional services marketers often overlook the obvious: superior client service. In a market where it is becoming easy for competitors to match technical service skills, pricing, distribution, and promotion, it may be that superior client service will be the only way for a professional service firm to differentiate itself. Although client management is a relevant tactic to consider for all four strategic options for growth (as discussed in Chapter Three), it is clearly more central to the implementation of a market penetration or market development strategy. In fact, client management will be instrumental for any professional practice wishing to maintain and build market share, either in their present market or through expansion into new geographic markets. The client management concept should be considered part of the practice philosophy for all or most professional firms. Client management is a tactical management tool that, in reality, is an umbrella for a number of activities. Thus, the key to understanding and implementing a client management program is to think comprehensively about the professional practice. Client management should be seen as a solution to managing and overcoming the difficulties caused by the Four I's of professional services (intangibility, inventory, inconsistency, and inseparability).

The four basic elements of any client contact management program include impression management, internal marketing, relationship marketing, and synchromarketing. Clients of professional services are becoming more demanding and the best professional services suppliers realize that service quality may be the only way to differentiate themselves in a relatively homogeneous industry. The skills and knowledge of professionals and their employees that influence the end result of the service are often referred to as "technical service quality." The appearance, behavior, customer orientation, and service mindedness of professionals and their employees is called "functional service quality" (Gronroos, 1985). The physical environment where the service is delivered and the ability to build a relationship with the client are also part of functional service quality.

Thus, clients do not evaluate the results of the service production process only (what they received), they also evaluate how they received it. In other words, it is not what is done (technical quality), but how it is done (functional quality) that makes the difference to the client. The coordination and management of technical and functional quality is required to be successful in professional practice in the 1990s. In order to ensure that quality service is delivered, those in professional practice must integrate all the elements of client management in a comprehensive and mutually reinforcing way.

A client management program can ensure that a professional service firm delivers client satisfaction which will result in greater profitability. In order to do so, senior management of professional firms must demonstrate their support for such a program. We will examine each of the elements of client management in greater detail and demonstrate how they can help overcome the problems caused by the Four I's.

IMPRESSION MANAGEMENT

Theodore Levitt (1981) suggests that services can rarely be tried out, inspected, or tested in advance. Prospective buyers are generally forced to depend on "surrogates" to assess what they are likely to receive from the service supplier. In essence, because of the intangibility of services consumers must rely on tangible evidence surrounding the professional service. A solution to the intangibility problem is impression management. Impression Management theory (Upah, 1983) holds that the ways in which clients come in contact with professional services firms are many and varied. Management of these "contact points" or tangible evidence is imperative if a firm is to convey the appropriate image. The key aspects of impression management that every professional firm should be conscious of are as follows:

1. Recognize that "everything about a service talks."
2. Clients evaluate what they cannot see by what they can see.
3. The impressions created at any contact point influence the perception of the service itself.
4. Impression Management requires a totally integrated approach to everything that communicates.

Professional services firms must integrate, manage, and coordinate all the contact points or evidence and do it better than their competitors. Upah (1983) suggests that there are basic contact points or evidence that must be managed by all professional firms:

1. *Physical Environment* — The ultimate goal is to create an environment or situation that produces the desired client impression and perception of professional service quality and leads to fulfillment of business goals. The physical environment of a service organization includes exterior and interior decor, accoutrements, music, furnishings, equipment, and color language.
2. *People* — Elements of this aspect of impression management involve the managing of the appearance and demeanor of the professional service providers and providing evidence of capability of performance (e.g., degrees, certificates).
3. *Procedures and Methods* — Procedures and methods used in the process of professional service delivery will influence

perceptions about the quality of the service. The design of procedures should be keyed to client needs and expectations and the overall service concept.

4. *Organizational Capabilities* — Tangible, objectively verifiable evidence as to a firm's capacity is often used by clients to evaluate a professional service organization. Such tangible evidence would include: years in operation, size, client list, demonstration of results achieved for other clients, and experience.

5. *Communications* — All communications should be designed to create the proper impression of the professional service firm. This includes written as well as oral communications. The quality and design of written communications have proven to affect readership and thus can favorably influence clients. The reality of the service should not be diluted by advertising that is too abstract. It is important to characterize the professional service firm via tangible elements and symbols, but the desired personality of the service organization should also be communicated. The personality conveyed should be consistent with the target group's expectations.

One way to view the impression management concept is shown in Figure 4-1. This figure shows some critical contact points which must be managed by the professional firm. The figure reveals that the client will assess all the information he or she is confronted with and then end up with an overall net impression of the professional service.

Professional services marketers must really put themselves in their clients' shoes, thinking through and gaining control of all the inputs to the consumer's mind that can be classified as contact points or tangible evidence of their service. Some may seem trivial until one realizes the impact they can have on service perception. To the client perception is reality.

For example, examine something quite simple like the colors

used in professionals' offices. Figure 4-2 shows the perceptions and associations a consumer can make simply by viewing certain colors. Think about how a client would view a practice if the interior color of the office was red versus blue. Too often colors are selected without regard for what the client may like or what the client may think of the professional as a result of the color language used in the offices. Generally, colors can be thought of in terms of warmth or coldness. For example, red, yellow, and orange are considered warm colors and as such tend to stimulate, excite, or create an active looking environment. Cold colors such as blue tend to provide an ice impression.

FIGURE 4-1. Impression Management — Contact Points

A. BUILDING EXTERIOR

• Appearance
• Signage
• Parking
• General neighborhood
• Other businesses located nearby

B. INTERIOR OFFICES

• Appearance
• Decor/color language
• Noise level
• Lighting
• Furniture

C. PROFESSIONAL STAFF

• Dress and general appearance
• Demeanor and attitude
• Telephone etiquette

D. SUPPORT STAFF

• Dress and general appearance
• Demeanor and attitude
• Telephone etiquette

E. OTHER

• Business cards and stationery
• Advertising and collateral materials
• Other clients served

A + B + C + D + E = NET IMPRESSION OF SERVICE

Referring back to the example of the red office versus the blue office, it is easy to see that a totally different impression of a professional practice can be derived by the client as a result of the color language used in an office. However, color language is not that simple; consider the use of blue. A dark blue tends to convey an image of trustworthiness and security, while mid-blue tends to convey an image of sobriety and sturdiness, and light blue tends to convey a sweetness or a calm or tranquil effect. The type of blue selected must therefore be considered in light of what image one would like to convey to the client. What this illustrates is that even something as simple as color selection for a professional's office should be considered part of impression management.

Another illustration of an important contact point is simply the reception the client receives on the telephone. The telephone is a critical contact point that can make or break a professional practice. Figure 4-3 depicts a basic guideline for handling the telephone in such a way that the proper image of the firm can be conveyed to current and prospective clients. One good way to receive unbiased feedback about how well a firm handles the telephone is to have a friend phone the office and ask what impression he or she had of the firm as a result of the phone call. Many professionals actually phone the office regularly just to spot check on the telephone etiquette of the firm.

INTERNAL MARKETING

The need for internal marketing in professional services firms is obvious. A professional services firm markets performances. These performances are, for the most part, delivered by people when the consumer is present. The quality level of those performances is important in order to attract and retain clients. Unfortunately, the quality of professional services may vary because of inconsistency and inseparability problems. In order to achieve greater consistency in professional services quality, and to overcome the problem of inseparability, internal marketing may be the answer. Internal marketing, as defined by Berry is:

> .... viewing employees as internal clients, viewing jobs as internal products, and then endeavoring to offer internal products that satisfy the needs and wants of these clients while addressing the objectives of the organization. (1980, p. 26)

FIGURE 4-2. Perception of Color

Red — Symbol of blood and fire. Brilliant and intense. Hottest color with highest action quotient. Most versatile color. Conveys strong masculine appeal.

Brown — Associated with earth, woods, mellowness, age, warmth, comfort. Another masculine color.

Yellow — Sunny, incandescent, radiant. Creates high impact to catch consumer's eye. Provokes a response of an active, cheering kind. Combined with red it equals a desire to conquer and the expectancy of something new.

Green — Symbol of health, freshness, nature, water. Greenish blue is a symbol of security and self-esteem.

Blue — The coldest color. Ice impression, sky, water. Dark blue can convey security; mid-blue conveys sobriety and sturdiness; light blue conveys calmness and tranquillity.

Black (and **Gold**) — Conveys sophistication, quality, ultimate surrender. Excellent as background or foil for other colors.

White — Spatial light, cool, snow, cleanliness. Conveys a youthful, frank, pure look.

FIGURE 4-3. The Telephone: A Critical Contact Point

1. Answer the phones with a positive and professional voice. Do it with a smiling face.
2. Never put a client on hold without asking for permission and waiting for his or her response.
3. Always check back with the client who is on hold.
4. Take down the message correctly; verify name and phone number of the caller.
5. Write down the message, with the time and date.
6. Answer the telephone by the third ring. If you are very busy ask someone to assist.
7. Get to know important clients (all clients are important but some are very important). Never give these clients the runaround.
8. Know the schedules of all the persons receiving calls so you can assist the caller by giving them calling times when the person is likely to be in.
9. Always answer the phone using the firm name, even after hours.
10. Always thank clients for calling.

Internal marketing starts from a notion that in order for a professional service firm to be successful it must treat its employees like internal clients. In essence, you cannot expect employees to show care and concern for their job or the clients unless they, as employees, are shown care and concern. Internal marketing can help a professional services firm attract and retain the best possible employees and get the best possible work from them. By satisfying the needs and wants of internal clients, a firm upgrades its capability for satisfying the needs and wants of its external clients.

In order to make an external market respond, the firm needs an acceptable product. The same is true for an internal market. A client-oriented and company-oriented attitude cannot exist unless the firm has something to offer its employees. A simple offering of a job with pay will not do it. A more market-oriented internal product is needed.

Thus, the internal product consists of a job and a work environment which motivates an employee to be client oriented. Management methods, procedures, personnel policy, training, and feedback all impact on the success of internal marketing programs. The first target group of any internal marketing program is top management, not contact personnel. If internal marketing is not accepted by management at that level it will not succeed. Moreover, the perceived quality of service of contact people is also affected by noncontact personnel. Such supporting personnel must also be included in an internal marketing program.

Berry (1980) argues that internal marketing involves creating an organization climate in general, and job products in particular, that lead to the right service personnel performing the service in the right way. In consumption circumstances in which people's performance is the product being sold, the marketing task is not only that of encouraging external clients to buy, but also that of encouraging internal clients to perform correctly. When they do, the likelihood of external clients continuing to buy is increased. Investing in the firm's staff through an internal marketing program is investing in service quality. A professional service firm cannot be client oriented if it is not employee oriented. Many professional firms have not considered this notion of internal marketing.

Many firms do not know what attitudes employees or support staff hold about their jobs, the organization, or management in general. One good way to examine the attitudes of these internal clients is to carry out a quality of work life survey. The survey is a way to gauge the employees' or support staff's perception and attitudes toward the job and the work environment. This should be done in order to determine or isolate any problems that may hinder or prevent the delivery of satisfaction to clients. Unhappy personnel can make unhappy clients.

Figure 4-4 depicts an example of a simple instrument that can be used to measure the quality of work life in a firm. Other information can be added to it, such as years of service, salary, or demographics, to determine if any differences in response can be attributed to those factors. It is recommended that this procedure be carried out annually.

If it is found that employees or support staff do not view their jobs as rewarding, or that they are worried about job security, or that they believe management is uncaring, there will be problems motivating them to focus on client satisfaction. But carrying

---

FIGURE 4-4.
Internal Marketing — Quality of Work Life Questionnaire

	SDA	DA	N	A	SA*
1. My job is worth doing and doing well.	1	2	3	4	5
2. I receive reasonable pay and benefits.	1	2	3	4	5
3. I feel I have job security.	1	2	3	4	5
4. I believe management is competent.	1	2	3	4	5
5. I receive feedback on job performance.	1	2	3	4	5
6. I have opportunity to learn and grow in my job.	1	2	3	4	5
7. I can get promoted based on merit.	1	2	3	4	5
8. The firm offers a good social climate.	1	2	3	4	5
9. The firm treats all employees fairly.	1	2	3	4	5
10. Management cares about their employees.	1	2	3	4	5
11. I enjoy my job.	1	2	3	4	5

*SDA = Strongly Disagree DA = Disagree N = Neither A= Agree SA = Strongly Agree

out the research should enable the firm to begin to address the issues of quality of work life within the professional practice. If problems are uncovered, the professional should be willing to take action. Such corrective action should be conducted in conjunction with the employees; they should be asked about what remedies they feel are warranted to affect change in the work environment. Having them participate in the decision-making process will ensure commitment to any new initiative designed to create a better working environment.

RELATIONSHIP MARKETING

Generating repeat business will be the key to success for professional services marketers in the 1990s. Relationship marketing should be viewed as a cultivation process, a way to ensure repeat business. The cultivation process posits a simple equation; greater involvement with the client leads to greater client commitment to the service which leads to greater loyalty. Berry defines relationship marketing as

> attracting, maintaining and enhancing client relationships. Servicing and marketing to existing clients is viewed to be as important to long-term marketing success as acquiring new clients. Good service is necessary to retain the relationship. Good marketing is necessary to enhance it. (1983, p. 25)

The objective of relationship marketing is to obtain and maintain clients by building a relationship with them. Attracting new clients should be viewed as only the first step in the marketing process. Ultimately, the professional service firm must build a relationship with that client and create loyalty. Upah (1983) suggests that relationship marketing can help tangibilize and differentiate the professional service, improve client management efforts, make the service more relevant and appealing, and as such, can help to solidify relationships, expand the relationship with the client, and reinforce what the professional service firm has done directly for the client.

It has been well established that it is much more cost-effective to retain clients than to go out searching for new ones. In fact, some research indicates that it may cost five times as much to replace a client as it does to retain one (*Marketing News*, 1991). Retaining clients is also important since satisfied clients not only remain clients but can be valuable generators of new business for the professional service firm. On the other hand, dissatisfied clients are lost clients and can be active agents working against the firm in generating new business. In fact, some statistics show that one satisfied client may tell one other client about the service while a dissatisfied one will tell between four and eleven prospects about their dissatisfaction with the service. Thus relationship marketing is vital not only to maintaining existing clients, but as a means to attract new ones.

Berry (1983) suggests there are a number of possible relationship marketing strategies that can be considered. Such strategies are not independent of each other and could be used in combination.

1. *Core Service Strategy* — A key relationship marketing strategy is the design and marketing of a core service around which a client relationship can be established. The ideal core service is one that attracts new clients through its needs-meeting character, cements the business through its quality, and provides a base for marketing additional services over time. For example, one small law firm specialized in fast, inexpensive will preparation. As a result of offering this core service and by doing it in an excellent manner, the firm was able to attract more business from those same clients in other areas of the law.

2. *Relationship Customization* — Another strategy is relationship customization. If a service firm can learn about the specific

characteristics of its clients it can more precisely tailor services to meet those specific needs. In doing so, the clients have an incentive to remain as customers rather than starting over with another supplier. The possibilities for relationship customization are considerable. Custom fitting the service to a client's particular requirements can be perceived as very valuable to the customer. One dentistry operation was able to determine that many patients wanted evening appointments and the option of a payment plan for dental work. In offering this service to those specific patients the firm was able to retain and attract patients.

3. *Service Augmentation* — Service augmentation involves building extras into the service to differentiate it from competitors' offerings. For service differentiation to occur, the extras must be genuine extras not readily available from competitors and ones that offer value to the client. The key is to build client loyalty since they should find these extras beneficial. If those extras are of value and not easily duplicated by competitors, then service augmentation can be a successful strategy. For example, an accounting firm which prepared corporate tax returns for small businesses offered, as part of its service, to prepare the individual tax returns for the owner/manager and any family members working for the small business.

4. *Relationship Pricing* — An old marketing idea — a better price for better clients — is the basis for relationship pricing. Relationship pricing encourages loyalty. In effect, clients are given a price incentive to consolidate their business with the professional service firm. This should be considered carefully for professionals whose governing bodies have established fee schedules.

The common element in all relationship marketing strategies is the incentive the client is given to remain a client. The incentive may be extras or a price break but in any case, the client is given one or more reasons not to change his or her professional.

SYNCHROMARKETING

One of the Four I's that can be very problematic for a professional services marketer is the inability to inventory service capacity. Idle capacity is always a problem in professional services marketing. But perhaps more difficult is the inability to handle peak load demands. This can cause problems when attempting to manage a relationship with a client. The synchronizing of demand and supply must occur in order to overcome idle capacity problems and to ensure client satisfaction.

The key in synchromarketing is adjusting supply to match demand and adjusting demand to meet supply. In other words, it means working both sides of the street. Altering the timing of consumer demand and/or exerting better control over the supply of the professional services offering is vital. The professional services marketer must avoid not only excess capacity but also situations where excess demand goes unsatisfied. This is particularly important when one considers valuable or highly profitable clients. It will be virtually impossible to build a relationship with such clients if they cannot be adequately serviced. In order to better match demand and supply, the following methods can be considered by professional services marketers:

1. Market similar services to target segments having different demand patterns.
2. Market service extras or price reductions during nonpeak times.
3. Train personnel to perform multiple tasks.
4. Hire part-time employees during peak times.
5. Educate consumers to use services during nonpeak times.

Communications can play a key role in synchromarketing. Use of media should be tied to capacity. Professional services marketers can communicate to clients about nonpeak times and encourage them to use the service during those times.

The fact that service extras or other incentives like price reductions are available at certain times can be communicated. It is also important to stop promotion or pull media when demand has already exceeded capacity. If an inability to meet peak load demands is causing dissatisfaction, demarketing may have to be used. What this means is that some low-profit clients may be using your service at peak load times and causing problems in delivering quality service to more valued clients. In this case, reducing demand from low-profit target segments that you do not want (or demarketing your services to them) may be necessary.

Remember that while you may want to provide quality service to all clients, some clients are just more important to your business than others. Focusing on ensuring that valued clients are satisfied with timely delivery of service is critical to success. The low-profit clients who may be price-sensitive may be receptive to using the service at nonpeak times if price reductions can be offered.

USING RESEARCH TO DEVELOP AND MAINTAIN A CLIENT MANAGEMENT PROGRAM

Too often professionals believe they know what their clients want and fail to deliver what those clients really need. This negates the possibility of building a relationship with them. In order to be successful in building relations with clients the professional firm needs to (1) measure customer needs and service attributes sought and (2) measure the firm's actual performance in delivering service based on those needs and attributes. You must determine what it is that clients are really looking for and whether or not the firm does or can deliver it. As competition increases in the professional services fields, superior service to clients is being used as a major competitive advantage; a way to attract clients.

Increasingly, clients are demanding greater levels of service quality and are becoming more unlikely to accept poor service. So, a professional firm who wants to remain competitive must carry out *client research* (what do they want and when do they want it?) and then conduct *performance research* to measure the extent to which the firm delivers it (performance as measured by the client). In this way the professional service firm can uncover possible market opportunities and discover hidden service problems before client attrition becomes a problem. Remember, client management is not just about creating clients but retaining them.

Client research and firm performance research can be simple and inexpensive or complex and expensive. Either way the professional service firm needs to:

1. Discover clients' needs.
2. Pinpoint the attributes clients are looking for when selecting professional firms.
3. Analyze how well the professional service firm measures up on those attributes and how well the firm performed in delivering service and satisfaction.
4. Determine what else the firm can do to increase satisfaction or build a better relationship with the client.

A simple client research instrument designed to examine the firm's service performance can be seen in Figure 4-5. This instrument does not measure the attributes being sought by the client but illustrates some of the attributes that may be important and how to measure just how well the professional service firm scores in terms of delivering on those attributes. Each firm should first uncover the clients' needs and the attributes that are

FIGURE 4-5. Service Performance Measurement Instrument

Dear Client.....Could you please take a few minutes and complete this instrument. Answer each question the way you feel best describes your experience and feelings with our service. For example, in question #1, a score of 5 would indicate complete agreement with the question that the firm's atmosphere was warm and friendly. Please circle one response per question. You are a valued client and we hope that this information can assist us with improving our service for you.

Atmosphere was cold and unfriendly	1	2	3	4	5	Atmosphere was warm and friendly
I received discourteous service	1	2	3	4	5	I received courteous service
I received incompetent service	1	2	3	4	5	I received competent service
Service was slow	1	2	3	4	5	Service was prompt
Staff were not helpful	1	2	3	4	5	Staff were helpful
Staff dressed poorly	1	2	3	4	5	Staff dressed well
The offices were dirty	1	2	3	4	5	The offices were clean
My problem was not solved	1	2	3	4	5	My problem was solved
Overall I am dissatisfied with the service received	1	2	3	4	5	Overall I am satisfied with the service received

important in delivering satisfaction, and then design an instrument similar to the one found in Figure 4-5 to measure the firm's performance.

WHAT CLIENTS REALLY WANT FROM PROFESSIONAL SERVICES PROVIDERS

What do clients generally want from professional services providers? Extensive research has shown that regardless of the professional service a client is using, there are three basic things a client wants from a professional:

1. Care and concern
2. Problem solving
3. Recovery

While some professional service firms may conduct client research and uncover different attributes, assume for now this is what most clients want from the professional service provider. They do want problem solving; this is why they are using the service in the first place. The role of a professional is to be a problem solver. Clients want the professional to be responsive and available, but primarily he or she has been selected to help them or fix them. Clients are also saying that in the course of solving their problem they want care and concern; they want a demonstration that the professional empathizes with them and really wants to help.

In fact, many experts believe that care and concern tends to rank even higher than problem solving as an attribute being sought by the client. Care and concern is not enough, however, if problem solving has not occurred. Conversely, it is important to remember that just solving the problem is not enough; how it is solved is a major factor in determining client satisfaction.

While some would argue that clients are not very forgiving in terms of the professional's ability to solve problems, most clients realize that occasionally something will go wrong. Sometimes a job took longer than planned, sometimes an employee was not as responsive or courteous as s/he should have been, or sometimes the firm just failed to give clients what they needed. Clients are prepared to forgive a bad performance if the professional service firm can recover and right the wrong. Prompt and effective recovery from a bad performance is what can salvage the relationship with the client. If something does go wrong with the delivery and performance of the service, there are a few basic principles that should be followed in order to correct the situation and save the relationship. Figure 4-6 outlines a basic guide for handling this critical aspect of client management.

Client management may be the difference between success and failure in professional services marketing. With time, energy, and some money, a client management program can be implemented that can offer the opportunity to excel in professional practice.

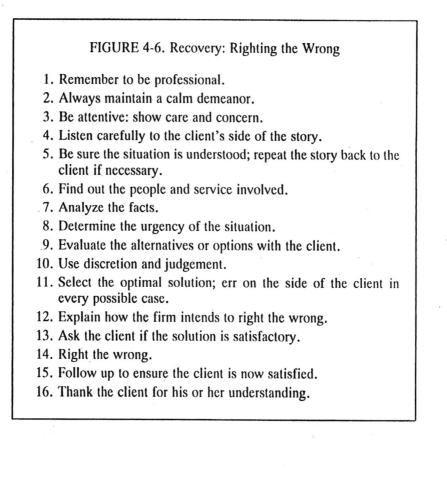

FIGURE 4-6. Recovery: Righting the Wrong

1. Remember to be professional.
2. Always maintain a calm demeanor.
3. Be attentive: show care and concern.
4. Listen carefully to the client's side of the story.
5. Be sure the situation is understood; repeat the story back to the client if necessary.
6. Find out the people and service involved.
7. Analyze the facts.
8. Determine the urgency of the situation.
9. Evaluate the alternatives or options with the client.
10. Use discretion and judgement.
11. Select the optimal solution; err on the side of the client in every possible case.
12. Explain how the firm intends to right the wrong.
13. Ask the client if the solution is satisfactory.
14. Right the wrong.
15. Follow up to ensure the client is now satisfied.
16. Thank the client for his or her understanding.

SUMMARY

1. Client management is essential for professional services firms who want to survive and to increase profitability. It may be the only way to achieve a competitive advantage in a competitive and maturing market.

2. Client management involves: (1) impression management, (2) internal marketing, (3) relationship marketing, and (4) synchromarketing. It can be used to overcome the problems caused by the Four I's of professional services marketing (intangibility, inventory, inconsistency, inseparability).

3. Both technical and functional professional service quality can be achieved through a comprehensive client management program. Remember it is not what you do, it is how you do it.

4. Remember the client's perception is reality so the professional must be certain the appropriate image is being conveyed to the client. Impression management involves the coordination and control over all the ways in which a client comes in contact with the firm. It requires attention to detail in the physical environment, people, procedures and methods, organizational capabilities and communications.

5. If the professional practice is employee-driven there should be no problem in successfully satisfying clients' needs. Employees and support staff must be treated like internal clients (internal marketing). A quality of work life instrument is a good starting place for embarking on an internal marketing program.

6. Relationship marketing is vital to success. Cultivating and building a relationship with clients will increase client satisfaction and loyalty. Four relationship marketing strategies are: (1) core service strategy, (2) relationship customization, (3) service augmentation, and (4) relationship pricing.

7. It is important to ask satisfied clients to actively refer services to friends and coworkers. More important, dissatisfied cli-

ents must be asked to tell the professional about their dissatisfaction first, rather than their friends.

8. Synchromarketing must be used to overcome the idle capacity problem prevalent in professional services marketing. More importantly, it can ensure that valued clients receive quality service on a timely basis. In order to better match supply and demand the professional services marketer can: (1) market similar services to target segments having different demand patterns, (2) market service extras or price reductions during nonpeak times, (3) train personnel to perform multiple tasks, (4) hire part-time employees during peak times, and (5) educate consumers to use services during nonpeak times.

9. In order to effectively implement a client management program some research must first be done to (1) identify and understand clients' needs and (2) then carry out a performance measure on how well the professional serves those needs.

10. A professional is hired to solve problems, but must always remember that behind every problem solved there is a client who must be shown care and concern. Occasionally, there will be problems in delivering quality professional service. When this happens the professional must recover and salvage the relationship with the client.

REFERENCES

Berry, Leonard L. "Service Marketing is Different," *Business*, Atlanta: Georgia State University, Atlanta, May-June, 1980, pp. 25-26.
Berry, Leonard L. "Relationship Marketing," in *Emerging Perspectives on Services Marketing*, Leonard L. Berry, G. Lynn Shostack and Gregory D. Upah (eds.), Chicago: American Marketing Association, 1983, pp. 25-28.
Gronroos, Christian. "Internal Marketing: Theory and Practice," in *Services Marketing in a Changing Environment*, Thomas M. Bloch, Gregory D. Upah and Valarie A. Zeithaml (eds.), Chicago: American Marketing Association, 1985, pp. 41-47.
Levitt, Theodore. "Marketing Intangible Products and Product Intangibles," *Harvard Business Review*, May-June 1981, pp. 94-102.

Marketing News. "Satisfaction-Action to Offer Tips on Pleasing Customers," Chicago: American Marketing Association, February, 4, 1991, p. 4.

Upah, Gregory D. "Impression Management in Service Marketing: Key Research Issues," in *Emerging Perspectives on Services Marketing*, Leonard L. Berry, G. Lynn Shostack and Gregory D. Upah (eds.), Chicago: American Marketing Association, 1983, pp. 105-107.

Chapter Five

Promoting Professional Services

There has been a tradition against the use of promotion in marketing professional services. Professional codes of ethics have often prevented the effective use of promotion. The main arguments against the promotion of professional services are (1) that promoting professional services will demean the professions, (2) that promotion will adversely affect consumer confidence in the professions, and (3) that promotion may even threaten the quality of professional services. Recently, however, bans against promotion have been relaxed or abolished. What has happened as a result? The use of promotion is seen in medicine, optometry, accounting, law, and other professions. Research has indicated that the much feared debasement or consumer negativity against the professions has not occurred, nor has any substantial evidence surfaced that the quality of professional services has diminished. For many professional associations, the issue now is how to assist members to use promotion in an effective and responsible manner.

In today's competitive marketplace, professionals cannot make the mistake of assuming there is no need to promote their services. Since professional services are intangible, professionals must tangibilize the services' existence. Promotion is one way to do so; it is now a key element of the marketing mix for professional services.

While some professionals are promoting their services inappropriately or in bad taste, promotion, when used properly, can be effective in establishing and expanding a professional services organization. This chapter will discuss the basic elements of the promotional mix as well as each element in detail. It will also offer guidelines for the effective use of promotion when marketing professional services.

THE PROMOTIONAL MIX

The promotional mix available to professional services marketers includes *personal selling, advertising, sales promotion, publicity,* and *word-of-mouth promotion.* This mix can be used to create demand or to project an image. Professional services marketers will need to use a combination of demand-oriented and image-oriented promotion. In general, all of the elements of the promotional mix can be used to:

1. Inform prospective clients about the benefits of the service.
2. Encourage them to try the service.
3. Remind them later about the benefits they enjoyed by using the service.
4. Develop and maintain a favorable corporate image.
5. Differentiate the service and the organization.

The professional services marketer can choose a combination of one or more of the promotional alternatives. Very often the professional services marketer will require use of all the elements of the promotional mix. However, some are more effective in achieving certain objectives than others. The professional must consider what has to be achieved and then select the appropriate promotional tool to accomplish it.

Promotion objectives can be established to impart information, to persuade, to remind, to differentiate the service, or to develop or maintain image. Each of the elements of the promotion mix will be discussed and related to how well they can achieve the aforementioned objectives.

Personal Selling

Personal selling involves face-to-face communication between the service provider and the client. Professionals need to apply effective sales techniques. Central to this is the ability of the professional to identify the needs of the client. Additionally, the professional must communicate to the client that he or she can offer a service that satisfies the client's needs. Research indicates that client satisfaction is influenced by the professional's attitude, personality, and ability to be sensitive to the client's needs.

There are certain advantages and disadvantages to the use of personal selling in professional services. The advantages of personal selling are:

1. The professional can control to whom the sales presentation is made.
2. The professional sees/hears the client's reactions and obtains feedback.
3. The professional can detail or provide complex information to the client.
4. Personal selling can be very persuasive.

The disadvantages of personal selling are:

1. It can be very expensive (on a cost-per-contact it is the most expensive).
2. Different professionals may change or offer different messages to clients.

One of the things that must be remembered by a professional who uses personal selling is that hard-sell or insistent selling is not advisable. A professional must understand the client's needs and offer the service to meet the needs, but should not oversell services or sell services the client does not need.

Personal selling is relatively expensive and inefficient if the primary objective of promotion is to inform a large number of clients that the professional service organization exists. It is more appropriate if the objectives of promotion are to detail the client and encourage the client to consume the service. Personal selling is also important as a follow-up to service consumption—personal contact after consumption can increase satisfaction with the service. Therefore, personal selling does play a role if the promotional objective is to remind.

Personal selling can also be used to develop and maintain image and to differentiate the service. Good personal selling contributes to the overall image of the professional service firm. Clients may judge the quality of the organization based on their experience during the sales process. In terms of differentiation, personal selling can help if the professionals and staff are courteous, efficient, and attentive to the client. Good personal selling efforts can encourage satisfied clients to positively recommend professional services providers. In today's market professionals must actively market their services in addition to being service processors. Because of the importance of face-to-face communication in professional services marketing this topic is dealt with in detail (see Chapter Eight).

Advertising

Advertising is a paid form of nonpersonal communication about the professional service organization or its service. Advertising involves mass media such as TV, radio, newspapers, and magazines.

There are several advantages to a professional services firm using advertising:

1. It can be attention-getting.
2. The firm can control what it says and when.
3. All clients and potential clients receive the same message.
4. It is efficient in reaching a large number of people.

The disadvantages of advertising are:

1. The cost of production and placement.
2. There is difficulty receiving good feedback.
3. People may be skeptical of the advertising claims.

Advertising may be the most effective promotional tool to use if the promotional objective is to inform a large number of people about the service. Advertising plays an important role if the promotional objective is to remind clients and to achieve an image development or maintenance objective.

Advertising can also play a major role in differentiating the professional service in the minds of consumers. While advertising is not as persuasive as personal selling, taken together these two elements can be powerful tools in informing clients about the service, projecting an appropriate image, reminding clients about the service, and creating differentiation.

Firestone (1983) as well as other services marketers suggest several roles that advertising can play in marketing services.

1. *Advertising can create the organization's world in the mind of the customer.* Advertising can describe the organization, its services, and its values. Advertising can tangibilize otherwise intangible services. The attributes of professional services can be demonstrated through advertising.

2. *Advertising can build and project an appropriate personality for the professional services firm.* Advertising can strike an emotional or cerebral response with the consumer. A professional service firm needs to be concerned with what a consumer

thinks of it but also how the consumer feels about the firm. Advertising can demonstrate a personality that will make consumers think well of and feel good about the professional service firm.

3. *Advertising can identify the professional service firm with the client.* The professional service firm will be successful if clients can relate the image and attitude of the firm to their needs and values. Advertising can create a bond between the professional service provider and the client.

4. *Advertising can influence how personnel handle clients.* Advertising can show the employees how they should deal with clients, how to be motivated to perform, and how to feel good about the organization.

5. *Advertising can warm up prospects for personal sales efforts that need to be undertaken.* Advertising creates awareness and interest but does not generally close deals. Advertising can create favorable customer predispositions toward the firm and as such can assist any personal sales efforts that may be made by the firm.

Professional services advertising also needs to provide tangible clues about the service, help in building favorable word-of-mouth exchanges, be consistent, and assist in reducing post-purchase anxiety. Advertising should be truthful and develop reasonable client expectations about the professional service.

Clearly, one of the most important aspects of advertising professional services is the need to emphasize the benefits of the services. Benefits need to be stressed and must be consistent with the benefits being sought by the client. The focus should not be on technical details but rather on how the client will benefit from the service.

Sales Promotion

Cowell (1984) suggests that services marketers dismiss sales promotion as part of the promotion mix far too quickly. While some argue that sales promotion is not an important promotional tool, he suggests that this is not true. Certainly some kinds of traditional sales promotions are inappropriate for professional services marketers, for example the sampling of a dentist's services. Ethical constraints may limit the use of this and other sales promotion activities. But many professionals use sales promotion, often under the guise of another name. A management consultant who offers an initial consult for free is using sales promotion. There are also other sales promotion activities that are considered appropriate for professional services marketers. For example, event or corporate sponsorship may be a very reasonable sales promotion activity that can be deployed by professionals. Particularly important would be grassroots involvement in community-based activities that create goodwill and visibility.

Cause-related marketing (covered later under publicity) can have a sales promotion component to it. Because of the inability to store capacity and the possibility of idle production capability, a sales promotion involving off-peak pricing schemes can be used by professional services. If sales promotion is to be used by the professional it should be integrated with the overall promotional mix and fit the image to be projected by the professional.

Publicity

Publicity is considered to be a nonpersonal, indirectly paid presentation of the professional service organization or its services. It can take the form of a news story, editorial, or service announcement. By using publicity the professional services organization attempts to get a medium to run favorable stories on the organization. The most common publicity tools are the news release or the news conference. However, often professionals will schedule speaking engagements in an attempt to obtain positive publicity.

There are some advantages of publicity:

1. Publicity is considered to be more credible than advertising.
2. Publicity involves little or no expense.

There are also some disadvantages:

1. It is difficult to obtain media cooperation.
2. There is little control over what is said, to whom, and when.

Publicity is rarely the main component of a promotional mix. However, it can help if the promotional objective is to impart information about the organization or its services. It may also play a role in reminding clients of the firm and in developing or maintaining image.

A relatively new form of publicity is cause-related marketing (CRM). Often it involves a professional service organization working with a charitable organization. The professional service organization may sponsor a charitable group or may be involved in fund-raising activities. CRM often wins much free publicity for the sponsoring professional services firm and helps in developing and maintaining the image of the firm.

Professional services marketers must always remember that good publicity is always planned publicity. If publicity is to be used as part of the promotional mix it should be planned for and integrated into the promotional budget and the promotion plan. For smaller professional services firms with limited marketing budgets, publicity can be an inexpensive way to gain exposure in the marketplace.

Word-of-Mouth Promotion

While some argue that since word-of-mouth promotion is largely beyond the control of the professional services marketer it should not be considered as part of the promotional mix. However, research indicates that consumers tend to rely more heavily on personal sources of information when selecting professional services than nonpersonal sources such as advertising (Crane, 1989). In fact, consumers prefer to use, and have more confidence in, personal referral or recommendations from existing clients of professional services suppliers.

While word of mouth is not systematic, research does show that negative word of mouth can travel five to ten times as fast as positive word of mouth. What this means to the professional is that if clients are unhappy with the professional service rendered they may tell others and this can negate all the good advertising in the world. On the other hand, positive personal referral can help strengthen the messages delivered through personal selling or advertising. What is said via word of mouth about the professional service organization can have positive or negative consequences on the growth potential for the operation. Professional services marketers can take greater control over word-of-mouth promotion by actively listening to what clients say to them and to others.

Professionals can encourage positive word of mouth, for example, by (1) inviting clients and prospectives to open houses, (2) networking with other professionals who can refer the firm's services, and (3) by simply asking satisfied clients to actively refer their services. Additional tactics could include (4) the development of materials for clients to pass along to prospects and (5) advertising to opinion leaders who can help spread the word about the service.

When putting the promotional mix together, the professional services marketer must always consider what objectives are to be achieved and the target market he or she is attempting to reach. The elements of a good promotion plan are shown in Figure 5-1. It is particularly important for professional services providers to construct an integrated plan. All elements of the promotional mix should be mutually reinforcing and project a consistent message and image to current and potential clients. Professional services providers would be well advised to prepare in advance their promotional activities and to detail them in a comprehensive calendar of events noting media to be used, times, and costs.

FIGURE 5-1. Elements of a Good Promotion Plan

1. Specific promotional objectives.
2. Details on the target market.
3. Breakdown of the promotional mix.
4. Specific message determination.
5. A detailed budget.
6. A calendar of events/activities for the year.
7. Evaluation and control measures.

PRODUCT (SERVICE) VS. CORPORATE ADVERTISING

The concept of corporate advertising has received greater attention over the past decade. However, there is confusion over what constitutes corporate advertising. Some consider corporate advertising as image or identity advertising. Others suggest corporate advertising as market preparation advertising. In this case, corporate advertising sells the organization behind the product and paves the way for product advertising. Corporate advertising can and should play a role in professional services marketing.

Earlier the concepts of demand-oriented and image-oriented

promotion were introduced. Corporate advertising plays a key role in image-oriented promotion. Corporate advertising is strictly soft-sell while product (service) advertising is generally demand-oriented. Because of the intangibility of the professional service, corporate advertising provides clues or cues about the service organization and can offer the client the opportunity to judge the organization as well as the service offering. In professional services marketing where services and service providers are seen as similar or undifferentiated, corporate advertising can create a perception of difference. In fact, research shows that if products are similar, corporate advertising can be used as a tie breaker; the professional service firm with the better corporate image as demonstrated through advertising will have a distinct advantage.

Determining objectives will dictate the appropriate use of corporate and product (service) advertising. If the objectives are awareness and image development, corporate advertising takes priority. If a firm is attempting to generate demand, then more product-oriented advertising is required. The professional services marketer will probably require a combination of corporate and service advertising in today's marketplace. Many times it is possible to integrate elements of both in specific advertisements.

Remember that to the consumer, who cannot see the service, the organization represents the service. Also, it should be noted that employees can be an important target for corporate advertising. Corporate advertising can also be used in reaching and motivating your employees to perform.

GUIDELINES FOR TELEVISION ADVERTISING

Television can be an important medium if the objective of the professional services marketer is to inform a large number of potential clients about the service offering. Television can offer broad reach and an opportunity to demonstrate the service creatively and tangibly. It can be a compelling medium. However, there are competing messages, often referred to as clutter, and television provides little selectivity. In other words, you may reach people who are of little interest to you. Also, television is not deemed as a credible source by many consumers. In fact, of all the media, consumers have the greatest skepticism toward television.

Since professional services are considered a high-involving and high-risk purchase, television may not have the credibility required to deliver your message. However, it can be considered as part of an overall promotional campaign. It can create awareness and may be appropriate for achieving this objective, while personal selling, for example, can be used for detailing and closing. If television is being considered as part of your promotional campaign, the following guidelines should be considered:

1. Television is a visual medium, so be visual. Demonstrate the benefits of the service.
2. Stick to a simple message and avoid a busy and overcrowded commercial.
3. It is critical to get the viewers' attention early. Audience attention does not build, so the first few seconds are vital.
4. Be sure that the corporate name is a central part of the commercial. It is necessary for prospective customers to remember a specific firm, not just a generic service being promoted.
5. It is important to convey some sense of who and what the professional is. The commercial should reflect a personality and image. Make sure it is possible to live up to the personality and image in the ad.

GUIDELINES FOR RADIO ADVERTISING

It is unlikely that any professional service firm would use radio as a primary medium (one that accounts for 50% or more of the promotion budget). But radio can be considered a good secondary medium when used appropriately. It is relatively inexpensive and frequency (number of times a client is exposed to a message) can be achieved quickly.

Radio is a portable medium and offers the advantage of immediacy of message. However, since it is not a visual medium it is difficult to create impact. There is also a lot of commercial clutter on the air and the message decays quickly. However, there are a few basic rules to follow if radio is being considered by the professional services marketer.

1. Try to create a picture of the service and organization in the mind of the consumer. Use a good combination of voice and sound.
2. Stick to one main selling point and deliver it clearly.
3. Like television, there is a need to capture the attention of the audience early.
4. Follow the old radio advertising axiom: tell them, tell them again, and tell them what you just told them. Be sure the firm's name registers with the consumer.
5. Use radio to get consumers to take action. Ask them to call or visit. Also, use radio to direct people toward other advertising you may be using (e.g., see our ad in the newspaper).

GUIDELINES FOR PRINT ADVERTISING

Electronic media (television and radio) is considered passive or low-involving media, while print (magazines and newspapers) is an active or high-involving media. Many professionals prefer print media primarily based on personal taste or preference. On a more objective basis, print is often the more appropriate medium for professional services because it is considered more credible than electronic media. Print offers some advantages over electronic media. It offers greater advertising permanence and good demographic and geographic selectivity. It is an excellent media if an informational campaign is being considered. There are special interest possibilities with print, especially magazines, and the potential for an editorially compatible environment.

There is also the opportunity to reach a good secondary audience because print tends to get passed along. Magazines offer good color reproduction potential but newspaper does not fare as well and color can be expensive in newspaper. Magazines require a long-term commitment and long closing dates. It is also difficult to build frequency through magazine advertising and it can be costly. If print is being considered, professional services marketers should consider the following guidelines:

1. Liberal use of pictures (preferably photographs) is recommended.
2. Simple and uncluttered layouts are required to obtain readership.
3. The headline should tell the story and the body copy should reinforce it.
4. Stick to a basic format for all print advertising including design, layout, and typeface.
5. Be information oriented. Print is a high-involvement media so you can use either a short-copy or long-copy strategy.

GUIDELINES FOR DIRECT MAIL

Contrary to belief, direct mail used correctly is not mass mail or junk mail. Direct mail can allow the professional to zero in on the target market being sought. It is the most focused of the media options. Direct mail is generally designed to be demand oriented. In fact, it is generally used when the objective is to have the consumer take direct action such as writing or phoning for information or making an appointment to discuss the service.

Direct mail is one of the fastest growing media in North America. It allows the advertiser to be very selective and to avoid waste. It can be personalized and professional services marketers can control the timing and format of direct mail. It also allows for effective measurement of results. With the rise in database marketing and mailing list brokering, direct mail can be an effective part of a sound promotion plan. It can bring new clients in, win back inactive accounts, collect accounts, research new service ideas, build goodwill, and warm up prospects for personal selling activity. In fact, direct mail with telemarketing follow-up has resulted in impressive growth in revenue for some services marketers.

But while direct mail can be effective, it is costly. Cost per exposure is one of the highest of all media types. Also, while at one time there was little worry about competition from other direct mail advertisements, the recent popularity of it has led to increased competitive activity. Because of the growth in direct mail, consumers are becoming irritated and often refuse to even look at it. Nevertheless, because direct mail can pay dividends its use will continue well into the future. The following guidelines should be considered if direct mail will be part of a promotional campaign.

1. Direct mail should be seen as a package consisting of several elements.
2. The envelope should arouse curiosity and begin the selling process.
3. The letter should be personalized as much as possible. Use the letter to interest the reader in the entire package.
4. The brochure or booklet should be the central piece.

5. A business reply envelope should be part of the package.
6. Make certain that the offer is tailored to the target market.
7. Use a copy strategy that stresses benefits to the client.
8. Get the client involved and active. Ask them to take the next step (e.g., call).
9. Test your elements including message, headline, type of envelope, paper stock, etc. before doing a full mailing.
10. Consider telemarketing as a possible follow-up to the direct mail effort.

PREPARING THE PROMOTIONAL MIX

There are many considerations in developing the optimal promotional mix. It seems that far too often cost drives the decision-making process. While cost is a factor, the ability of a promotional tool to reach a target market or its capacity to achieve a given promotional objective should be determinant factors.

Before an appropriate promotional mix is constructed the professional service provider must consider:

1. Who is the target market being sought and where are they?
2. What are the promotional objectives?
3. Which vehicles will achieve the desired objectives?
4. How much money is required (and available) to do the job?
5. How often should promotion be used?
6. What are the competitors doing? Are they spending more money?
7. Will clients be more receptive to some forms of promotion more than others?

SUMMARY

1. Promotion is a required and important part of the marketing mix for the professional services provider.

2. The promotional mix for the professional services marketer consists of personal selling, advertising, sales promotion, publicity, and word-of-mouth promotion.

3. Promotion can be demand oriented and image oriented and professional services marketers need to strike a balance between the two.

4. Promotion is used to inform, create demand, remind, develop, and build a favorable image and differentiate the service.

5. Personal selling must be an integral part of the promotional mix for a professional services marketer.

6. Advertising can be used to inform or remind large numbers of clients or prospects about professional services available.

7. Some sales promotional activities may be appropriate for professional services, particularly off-peak pricing and event or corporate sponsorship.

8. Publicity should be planned, controlled, and integrated into the promotional mix. Cause-related marketing (CRM) can be an effective publicity tool for professionals.

9. Word-of-mouth promotion is important to professional services marketers and can be encouraged through good advertising, by asking clients to actively recommend the service, networking with other professionals, and seeking out opinion leaders.

10. Elements of a good promotion plan include: (1) specific objectives; (2) detailed target market; (3) promotional mix breakdown; (4) message; (5) budget; (6) calendar of events; and (7) evaluation measures.

11. Both product (service) and corporate advertising are required for professional services marketing.

12. Use media wisely and refer to the guidelines offered in this chapter when using media as part of the promotional mix.

REFERENCES

Cowell, Donald W. *The Marketing of Services*, London: Heinemann, 1984.

Crane, F. G. "Choice Criteria and Cue Usage in Selecting Lawyers," *Journal of Professional Services Marketing*, (5)1, 1989, pp. 113-121.

Firestone, Sidney H. "Why Advertising a Service Is Different," in *Emerging Perspectives on Services Marketing*, Leonard L. Berry, G. Lynn Shostack and Gregory D. Upah (eds.), Chicago: American Marketing Association, 1983, pp. 86-89.

Chapter Six

Managing in a Professional Services Environment

Professionals often focus their efforts exclusively on providing services to their clients. However, in order to be successful in today's marketplace, the professional has to be concerned with managing a practice and employees as well. Professionals cannot manage by instinct or by the seat of their pants. A professional services organization can crumble as a result of poor management. In this chapter we will examine the fundamentals of managing in a professional services environment.

MARKETING AS A MANAGEMENT TOOL

In Chapter Four we discussed the relevance and importance of internal marketing. Since people are responsible for delivering professional services it is important to have motivated, service-minded, and productive employees. Proper management of people can go a long way in achieving organizational objectives. Marketing is all about exchange, as is much of what we know about management. In order to successfully carry out exchange activities, either with clients or employees, professionals must adopt a marketing perspective. Drucker (1973) has said that most of what we call management consists of making it difficult for people to get their work done.

This is because managers often manage by fear or anxiety; or are production-oriented not marketing-oriented. Figure 6-1 depicts the differences between a production-oriented and a marketing-oriented manager in a professional services environment. We will examine each of the differences in some detail.

FIGURE 6-1. Production versus Marketing-Oriented Manager
in a Professional Services Environment

Production-Orientation	**Marketing-Orientation**
• Production-Oriented	• Employee-Oriented
• Sells output to Employees	• Uses Consensus for Output
• One-Way Communication Process	• Two-Way Interactive Process
• Emphasis on Short-term Objectives	• Emphasis on Long-term Objectives
• Narrow view of employees needs	• Broad view of employees needs
• Little adaptation to environment	• Adaptation to environment
• Cost Oriented	• Profit Oriented

Production Orientation vs. Employee Orientation

Obviously, this author believes there exists a dichotomy between professionals who are production-oriented and those who are employee-oriented. A professional who is production-oriented is concerned with producing a service and not with the needs of the client. Similarly, the production-oriented professional-as-manager is a production pusher whose primary interest is in producing/completing the task at hand with little regard to his or her people. Just as professionals must be client-oriented, managers in a professional services environment must be people-oriented. Managers who make the transition from task orientation to people orientation can inspire and motivate employees to achieve collective objectives.

Sells Output to Employees vs. Uses Consensus for Output

Essentially, a production-oriented professional must rely on selling to get rid of product. If the product met the needs of clients, selling would not be necessary. Similarly, the production-oriented professional-as-manager assumes employees are basically incompetent or lazy or both and must be sold on the concept of working. Little regard is shown for employee input by the production-oriented manager. He or she tends to use the concept of hierarchical power to overpower adversaries, suppress conflict, and implement (sell) ideas. The marketing-oriented professional is one who exhibits concern for his or her people as well as completing the tasks at hand. Such a manager maintains positive relations and creates a healthy work environment through cooperation, interdependent teamwork, and a consensus-driven approach.

One-Way Communicative Process vs. Two-Way Interactive Process

Professionals who use a production orientation to manage believe communication is a one-way process: from them to the employees. To effectively complete the work that must be accomplished in a professional services organization there needs to be two-way communication. Feedback is critical to the communication process in locating problem areas and ensuring their resolution. Marketing-oriented managers know the process and accept it as a basic part of their everyday activity. Communication, to them, is incomplete without integrated feedback. Marketing-oriented managers seek out and encourage feedback from employees about all aspects of the professional practice.

Emphasis on Short-Term Goals
vs. Long-Term Goals

Production-oriented managers focus on the day-to-day tasks with little regard to the future. They adopt a crisis management philosophy which inhibits their effectiveness and efficiency. It is difficult for them to even evaluate where they are, not to mention coming to grips with where they are going or how to get there. On the other hand, those with a marketing orientation work from a well-grounded plan which provides direction for not only short-term activities but ultimately, for long-term achievement of organizational objectives. In essence, this allows the marketing-oriented manager to be proactive rather than reactive.

Narrow View of Employees
vs. Broad View of Employees

Production-oriented professionals view all employees as essentially the same. They have little regard for the individual needs and wants. Everyone is considered a homogeneous mass. A marketing-oriented manager recognizes the heterogeneity of people in developing products (jobs) or policies that will create satisfaction. This leads to more flexible forms of organizing and managing people. This approach is necessary in order to utilize individual talents to achieve organizational objectives.

Little Adaptation to the Environment
vs. Adaptation to the Environment

A production-oriented professional assumes people will accept whatever is offered or proposed. This type of person rejects change and falls into the corporate comfort trap; they continue to do as they have done. Those that are marketing-oriented seize opportunities, innovate, and adapt to changes in the internal and external environment.

There is evidence to suggest that the perception of work is changing in our society. There is a new, fresh acceptance of the work ethic. Workers are rejecting the concept of authoritative management. Jobs are becoming more important to people, as well as their satisfaction with them. Workers are seeking creative, action-oriented environments in which to work. The old style of management (fear and reward) is being rejected by employees in favor of intrinsic interests such as the pursuit of excellence and personal fulfillment. Employees are rejecting the manipulative, production-type manager who is more interested in pushing ideas than in satisfying their needs and wants. A marketing orientation will allow the professional-as-manager to understand and deal with the changing requirements of effective management.

Cost vs. Profit Orientation

To be marketing-oriented means to look beyond cost/sales to profitability. A manager in a professional firm that looks at the costs of carrying out tasks rather than the total impact of any given mode of operation is bypassing an opportunity to provide better overall efficiency for the firm. An overemphasis on cost reduction can cause lower satisfaction and negatively impact on future participation by both employees and others outside the organization that must live with such cost-cutting behavior. Marketing-oriented managers are able to grasp the big picture: that costs must be incurred in order to achieve objectives. Profitability is not seen just in a monetary sense but is viewed as the overall achievement of established objectives.

The acceptance of a marketing orientation is critical to the success of any product. Marketing can and should transcend every aspect of an organization. Production-oriented managers in a professional services environment who fail to accept a marketing perspective must surely go the way of the dinosaur. Paying attention to employees' needs is just as important as paying attention to clients' needs. It is easy to find organizational schizophrenia in professional services organizations. Management can talk about client satisfaction on one hand, but can neglect employee satisfaction. Success in professional services marketing requires you to be employee-driven as well as client-driven.

THE FUNDAMENTALS OF MANAGING IN A PROFESSIONAL SERVICES ENVIRONMENT

Internal marketing (Chapter Four) can only be operationalized through effective management. There are several fundamentals of managing in the professional services environment. We will examine each one in some detail.

Fundamental #1 — Practice the Art of Delegation

Knowing exactly when and how to distribute the workload in a professional services environment is a critical management skill. A professional must first accept that delegation has to be part of his or her management skills. Finding and then delegating responsibility to the right people are the next steps.

When delegating work the professional manager must be certain to delegate the entire job. Start-to-finish responsibility is a required part of delegation. It is also important to communicate to everyone in the firm the person to whom the work has been delegated. If no one is sure who is responsible to complete the tasks, they may remain undone.

It is necessary to assign good as well as bad tasks. Employees should share the unpleasant tasks. When delegating the professional manager should provide specific instructions and make certain his or her expectations are clear. Employees must be told when and how the job is expected to be completed. If possible expectations should be put in writing to avoid confusion. However, the employee must be allowed some latitude in completing the tasks. They may not complete the task the same way as the manager would, but they must be allowed to use their own style if the task can be successfully completed their way. Creative problem-solving in the professional services environment should always be encouraged and rewarded.

Fundamental #2 — Build a Team

Motivation is critical in marketing professional services. One way to motivate is to demonstrate to employees that they are part of a team. Show employees that they are valued and that their performance is critical to the success of the firm. Take the time to ask their input when making decisions; this will lead to commitment to the course of action decided upon. A well-organized and happy team will provide excellent service to a client every time.

Fundamental #3 — Be a Communications Specialist

Misunderstandings in a professional services environment can destroy team spirit and morale. Clear communication can help avoid such problems. Communicating effectively with employees is extremely important. Be specific and spell out exactly what you desire. Try in every case to speak to the employee directly and not through a third party. Ask the employee if he or she understands and encourage him or her to seek clarification if it is needed. It is important to hold regular meetings with the staff in order to communicate objectives and to obtain collaboration. The concept of communication is so important in professional services marketing we will discuss it in more detail in Chapter Eight.

Fundamental #4 — Lead by Example

Remain in touch with clients and employees. Be highly visible; show employees concern for the business, the clients, and themselves. Do the right things and be sure that employees see them being done. The professional should share his or her vision of the firm with the employees as often as possible. Learn to pull people along not push them along. Employees should never be asked to do something that the professional is not prepared to do. He or she must set the standards of performance and lead through excellence.

Fundamental #5 — Practice Servitude

A manager in a professional services environment needs to accept the role of serving the people who serve the clients. This is an extremely difficult concept for professionals to accept. It does not mean that strong leadership cannot be shown. In fact, being prepared to do the little things for clients and employees will go a long way in demonstrating the desired leadership.

TIME MANAGEMENT

Professionals are constantly engaged in a war against the clock. The time must be found to provide excellent professional service to clients on a daily basis, to manage, and to develop new business to ensure survival and growth of the firm. A professional's productivity often comes down to how well he or she manages their time. Professionals need to be organized and systematic in order to manage time wisely. However, few people have a system for using time effectively. This book cannot offer a canned solution or complete system for time management. However, here are some guidelines that can be used to manage time wisely, allowing for a more productive performance.

1. Prioritize Tomorrow's Tasks Tonight

Time should be taken every day to actually write down, in rank order of importance, what tasks need to be completed the next day. This provides for a focus on what needs to be accomplished every day. It also makes it possible to track how well tasks are being completed. Some tasks may not get completed that day. If not, the new task list should always include the uncompleted tasks from the day before on the top of the list. If uncompleted tasks are being carried over every day, productivity suffers. Soon the professional will become overwhelmed with having too many things to do and too little time to do them in. This is called time poverty, which can be damaging both emotionally and financially.

2. Avoid Time Wasters

Some habits and/or people waste valuable time. Some habits that are time wasters are television, oversleeping, procrastination, and negative thinking. The average adult watches twenty-five hours of television a week. This author rarely considers watching television an effective use of time. If a program has some relevance to one's occupation or industry then that may be fine. But watching mindless sitcoms is not a good way to spend valuable time.

Quite frankly, most people sleep too much. If a person sleeps eight hours a day he or she should consider sleeping seven and one-half hours. Working this extra half hour per day will add an extra month in productive time annually (182 hours extra $\div$ 40-hour work week = 4.5 extra weeks per year). If one can squeeze an extra month of time into each year, it should pay dividends personally and professionally.

Procrastination is deadly. Most people will not plan out their day or put it in writing because they know they will not follow it. Often people cannot get motivated to complete the tasks at hand so they avoid the tasks. Everything becomes more interesting than the one thing that must be completed.

Many professionals also get hung up because of negative thinking. Negative thoughts are draining and a waste of energy and time. Emotions such as jealousy, anger, and fear can derail a person. Learn to forget about things that cannot be controlled and focus on things that can. Time is one resource that can and must be controlled.

3. Follow Plans, Not Moods

Everyone has good days and bad days. However, moods should not be allowed to dictate performance and productivity. If tomorrow's tasks are prioritized tonight, transitory emotions should not be allowed to put one off course. One must organize and discipline oneself or herself to commit to the high priority tasks regardless of daily external/internal factors that can pre-empt one's performance.

4. Review and Improve the Schedule

Most professionals must have a daily schedule. The way time is scheduled can make or break the professional. An indication of a poor schedule is not staying on time. (As mentioned earlier in the book, the problem could be failing to prioritize tasks.) Keeping clients waiting is not a good practice. Another sign of a poor schedule is finding oneself totally drained during the day. It is necessary to be fresh and energized to be on top of one's job, but a poorly designed schedule can exhaust the professional. There is no one schedule that works best for everyone, nor one that can work across professionals. For example, some professionals such as dentists see clients in streams, whereas accountants generally do not. But there are a few things that can be done to improve a schedule. Most professionals have to complete routine paperwork and correspondence. They can set aside fifteen minutes in the early morning or at the end of the day to carry out these tasks. Many professionals also have to return routine phone calls and it is a good idea to set aside a time to complete these calls in a block.

Determine what other routine tasks must be done in the run of a day and calculate how much time these tasks require. If they are not generating revenue, try to complete them during nonrevenue-generating time. Also keep in mind that a crowded schedule may look good on paper but there should always be an empty block of time for emergencies or other matters that may crop up during the day. The empty time block also helps rescue the professional who does fall behind in his or her schedule. Some professionals use the empty time block (15-30 minutes) strictly for cultivating new business. They use the time to call or write to prospective clients, to network with other professionals, or to discuss cross-servicing with existing clients. If the professional can build this business development tactic into each day he or she should not have to worry about clients coming down the pipeline in the future. One of the most important things to remember about a schedule is that it should be personal; the person making it should control it. The professional should try to schedule activities, appointments, and meetings that make sense for him or her and communicate this to the staff so that they are aware of scheduling preferences.

5. Set the Agenda

Most professional working days get eaten up by trivial drivel and interruptions unless an agenda is set. Professionals cannot be driven by what other people deem is important. They need to view time as an opportunity for performing what they need to do in order to be successful.

SUMMARY

1. A professional needs to be a good manager. Proper management of people can help in achieving organizational objectives.

2. The professional-as-manager needs to be marketing-oriented to manage effectively. This means (1) being employee-oriented; (2) using consensus for decision making; (3) using a two-way communication process; (4) emphasizing long-term objectives; (5) taking a broad view of employees' needs; (6) adapting to the environment; and (7) being profit-oriented.

3. Effective management in the professional services environment also involves five fundamentals: (1) practicing the art of delegation; (2) building a team; (3) being a communications specialist; (4) leading by example; and (5) practicing servitude.

4. Professionals need to manage their time wisely. Basic ways to maximize time include: (1) prioritizing tomorrow's tasks tonight; (2) avoiding time wasters such as television; (3) following your plans, not your moods; (4) reviewing and improving your daily schedule; and (5) setting your own agenda.

5. Professionals need to be employee driven and client-driven in order to be successful in today's environment.

REFERENCE

Drucker, Peter F. *Management: Tasks, Responsibilities, Practices*, New York: Harper & Row, 1973.

Chapter Seven

Trade Area Analysis, Site Selection, and Facility Design

This chapter will examine the importance of conducting a trade area analysis when planning to locate a new professional services operation, as well as the need to complete a trade area analysis for an existing operation on at least an annual basis. The specific selection and reevaluation of an existing site within a given trade area will also be covered as well as facility design criteria.

TRADE AREA ANALYSIS

The location of a professional services operation, in most cases, is a serious and important decision. In order to be successful the professional services marketer must understand the nature of various geographic markets and the potential for business to be generated from those areas. There is little agreement among marketers as to what constitutes a trade area.

Stern and El-Ansany (1982) define a trade area from three perspectives: the buyer's, the seller's, and sales and/or volume. If the buyer's perspective is used, a trade area is the region inside which the buyer may reasonably expect to find the service conveniently located for personal consumption. If the seller's perspective is used, a trade area is the region whose size is determined by boundaries within which it is economical in terms of delivering the service. From the sales or volume perspective, a trade area is the area surrounding the professional services outlet from which ninety percent of sales or volume is derived. This may be confusing but the professional services marketer has to consider all three of these perspectives when dealing with the trade area issue. Obviously, when attempting to establish a business, the professional services marketer has to consider where it would be economical to do business and this is often contingent upon whether or not a large enough target market exists and whether or not the target market is prepared to do business there.

Additionally, the professional services marketer has to determine just what the physical boundaries will be for the trade area. In other words, what will be the size and shape of the trading area? This is particularly important when calculating market potential and when considering business expansion through multisite development (market development). A professional practice generally does not want to establish a new operation in a trade area served by an existing operation since this creates trade area overlap and possible cannibalization.

In the quest for a geographic location from which to do business, the professional services marketer needs to consider three key variables: (1) characteristics of the population, (2) economic factors, and (3) factors that contribute to the quality of life for those that live or work in the area. There are several factors that must be considered within each of the these categories. Figure 7-1 shows the factors that must be examined when considering a trade area.

One of the most important factors is the size of the target market available in the trade area. Another critical consideration is how saturated the market is. Is demand for the professional service equal, below, or above existing supply? Too often professional services marketers use intuitive judgment or personal bias during the trade area evaluation stage and select a trade area that is saturated, thus making it difficult to run a viable operation.

Market potential calculation must be made in the trade area and weighed against the ability of competitors to meet existing and/or future demand. This is not generally difficult to accomplish. It is very easy to obtain what the per capita expenditures are on particular professional services in a given trade area. If this is known and the size of the population is known, then overall market potential can be calculated. For example, say the average person spends $100 on dental services per year in trade area A. If the trade area population is 10,000, then the overall market potential in trade area A is $1 million for dental services. However, let's also assume that the trade area already has three dentists and, for illustration purposes, the average dentist requires $250,000 gross revenue to break even. The assumption is made that natural market share is at work in the trade area. That is, each dentist is receiving an equal market share. In this case, the average dentist is generating $333,000 per year ($1 million/3). This is above the break-even point and it can be assumed that each dentist has a viable operation. Assume that a new dentist decides to locate in that area anyway. If the assumption of natural market share is made, what would be the potential? In this case, by obtaining natural market share, each dentist would generate $250,000 which is the break-even point ($1 million/4). This trade area, unless it is growing at a fast rate, should be considered saturated. However, in business rarely does natural market share exist. Some professionals are just better than others (competitive advantage) and can generate unnatural market share. This means that it is possible to enter even a saturated trade area and still be successful. However, to achieve more than an equal share of market a professional must have a competitive advantage. It is often difficult to generate new demand for services so market share will and must come at the expense of competitors. However, most professionals may be advised to seek unsaturated markets first and work on market penetration in those trade areas simply because it may be less costly and involve lower risk. When considering trade areas, therefore, the size and possible growth of the target market sought as well as the existing competition should be key determinants for trading area selection.

FIGURE 7-1. Trade Area Variables

Population Factors

Distribution of age groups
Level of education
Percentage of home owners vs. renters
Size and rate of population growth
Gender
Social class and subculture

Economic Factors

Disposable Income
(Un)Employment rates
Retail sales potential
Tourism inflow
Labor availability

Quality of Life Factors

Availability of transit
Climate
Schools
Roads
Culture and recreational facilities
Police and fire protection

There are several factors that determine the size and shape of a given trade area for a professional service. One consideration is the type of professional service. Some professional services that are highly specialized will have the ability to draw clients from a greater distance than nonspecialized or commodity-based professional services. Another factor is the price of the professional service. If there is price competition for a certain professional service, a client may be prepared to travel farther for the better priced service thus creating a larger trade area. A third factor is the location and availability of competition. If there are few substitutes available, a trade area for a professional service may be quite large. However, if there are many competitors then it is likely that each competitor will share a smaller trading area. A final factor would be physical and psychological barriers to a trade area. A trade area may cut off potential clients because of a physical barrier (traffic congestion) or a psychological barrier such as being considered a high crime area.

When seeking to make decisions about trade areas, a professional services marketer should draw information from a variety of sources. Two useful sources from the U.S. Department of Commerce are the *County and City Data Book* and the *Statistical Abstract of the U.S.* Another source in the United States is the *Editor and Publisher Market Guide.* In Canada, *Statistics Canada* offers a variety of data that would be useful in assessing various trade areas.

For professional services marketers already in business, is there a need to conduct a trade area analysis for an existing operation? The answer is yes. Such an analysis will answer several questions:

1. What is the market potential in the current trade area? Is it growing or shrinking?
2. What is the professional's current share of market? Is it getting bigger or smaller?
3. Where are the clients coming from? How far are they travelling?
4. Can another site be operationalized to satisfy clients who are not currently using the existing site?

A very simple way to determine the extent of an existing trade area is to randomly select about 400 client files and to physically plot on a map where they live/work. If done properly, the resultant trade area will probably reveal the geographic boundaries from which about eighty to ninety of the clients are drawn.

SITE SELECTION

Once a decision is made on a general trade area, a specific site must be selected within the trade area to set up an operation. The question then is what part of the trade area should be selected? Should the operation be established in the central business district, in a shopping center, or in an isolated business location? Obviously, many of the factors that dictate the choice of the general trade area impact on the decision of where to specifically establish the business within the trade area. Some of the key factors, in addition to location of target market and competition can be seen in Figure 7-2.

FIGURE 7-2. Factors Affecting General Site Selection

1. Overall attractiveness and appeal of site
2. Adequacy of mass transportation and parking facilities
3. Traffic volume and pattern (pedestrian and vehicular)
4. Local ordinances and zoning regulations
5. Accessibility to the site
6. Compatibility of neighboring businesses
7. Costs and expansion potential

Each particular site within the trade area will have advantages and disadvantages. There may be more than one type of site situation available in the trade area and each should be analyzed as to which one would be best for the operation. Further, there may be more than one site within a particular building or buildings on a site. For example, there may be one site in the central business district and two sites within a particular shopping center. When analyzing individual site possibilities, several factors must be considered in addition to the general factors for site selection listed in Figure 7-2. These include (1) history of site and (2) conditions of immediate area around site. Before locating in a particular site it is advisable to seek information on the history of the site. Has there been another professional services operation there before? Was it successful? Why did it move? If the previous owner or tenant can be located it would be useful to obtain the answers firsthand. Talking to other business owners nearby is also advisable. It should be remembered that even if previous professional services marketers failed at this location before it does not imply that the new business will fail. However, consumers often have an image of a particular site and that is usually developed as a result of their experience with the business that occupied that location. If their experience has been negative, some negative carryover may exist.

Generally, professional services marketers cannot afford to own their building or dominate the immediate environment surrounding the operation. Thus, the professional services marketer must be concerned with the immediate area that will not be under his or her control. There are several factors that affect the quality of the area surrounding the professional services operation. They include (1) vacant sites and buildings, (2) poor walking areas, (3) hours of operation in area, and (4) location clutter. Empty stores cannot generate consumer traffic and can give the area a depressing appearance. If the professional services operation depends on consumer traffic, vacant sites and buildings will not help. Lack of sidewalks or poor sidewalks may inhibit consumer traffic. Also, anything blocking traffic flow on the sidewalk is problematic for the consumer.

The professional services marketer must examine the hours of operation of other businesses in the area. Many consumers prefer to do one-stop shopping and may only be willing to use the services if they can conveniently complete other shopping tasks at the same time. The final consideration is whether or not the consumer can see the location when approaching it. It is important to determine if the site is visible or hidden by satellite structures that may have built up around it. If the problem does not currently exist, it is advisable to determine if such developments are pending since the problem may arise in the future. The professional services marketer should always be future-oriented when selecting a trade area, a general site, and specific site location. The optimal location is one that can be operationalized easily in the short term but will also offer potential for growth and expansion in the future.

In order to increase the chances of success, the professional services marketer needs to select a business location that has a base of consumers to draw from. These consumers need to know that the service is available and that it is convenient, accessible, and appropriate for them to use. Often professional services marketers assume that the only costs clients incur when consuming professional services are the fees charged. However, there are many other costs connected to obtaining professional services such as the consumer's time to and from the location, as well as psychic and financial costs caused from inadequate or expensive parking and/or poor access to the location. The old axiom of business success used to be "location, location, location." This may not be totally true for professional services, but it is an important axiom to remember.

FACILITY DESIGN

The importance of impression management in marketing professional services was seen in Chapter Four. An important element of impression management is the physical environment from which the services are produced and rendered. While a nice looking physical environment cannot compensate for poor or inadequate service, it does send a message or a clue about the service to everyone who walks through the door. The physical environment can communicate the professional philosophy of the professional services marketer. A good physical environment should (1) make clients feel comfortable, confident, and safe; (2) communicate a sense of pride in the professional services operation; and (3) be a reflection of the quality of professional services that are offered.

Environmental psychologists have long argued that the physical environments where people work promote and display who they are and what they think of themselves. Chapter Four showed how something as simple as color language can enhance or inhibit professional image. Physical appearances allow the consumer to make judgments about the professional services under consideration. Every piece of the physical environment such as signage, building exterior, and building interior can provide a positive or negative impression to the consumer. As part of the marketing audit, the professional services marketer should examine physical facilities critically. Does the physical environment tell the consumer who the professional is, what he or she does, and how well it is done? If not, changes in the physical environment may be in order. Many professionals are reluctant to make changes in their physical environment because it involves both time and money. There are other reasons why professionals may not be interested in making changes to their physical surroundings. First, many are happy with the status quo and incapable of being objective about their surroundings. The professional often does not see the environment the way the client does and thus does not see the reason to make changes. Second, many professionals see the need for changes but lack the energy or ideas to make the changes. And third, many professionals believe that clients pay for professional services not for superficial elements such as a designer-built office. But a professional must remember that the consumer may view the physical surroundings as a logical extension of the professional. It is possible that some consumers may react negatively to the professional's physical surroundings and not wish to consume the service.

When evaluating the environment the professional must consider not only the clients but the employees. A good physical setting can help motivate personnel and maintain productivity. The physical environment must be assessed ergonomically and from an atmospherics perspective. When applying ergonomics and atmospherics to a professional's physical environment the following must be considered:

1. *Lighting* – To assist personnel in completing their tasks adequate lighting is required. Employees as well as clients will benefit if a view of the outdoors is available.

2. *Acoustics* – Noise can be distracting and disturbing to both employees and clients. It can also negatively impact on professional image. Anything that can be done to reduce internal and external noise should be undertaken, including installing acoustic tile and carpeting.

3. *Temperature* – Both personnel and clients need to be comfortable in the physical environment. Temperatures between 65° and 75° F are suggested for an office environment, and humidity should be less than 50 percent.

4. *Music* – Good background music can relax clients as well as offer cover for private conversation. The proper tempo of music is important since music that is too fast may create client anxiety.

5. *Color* – The selection of color in a professional office is important. Color can set the tone and mood of the office. Remember color has an emotional impact on clients and em-

ployees. Determine what mood is desired and select colors accordingly.

6. *Patterns of movement* – Employees and clients should be able to move easily in the physical environment. An ideal traffic flow needs to be part of the environment. Recently, a circular arrangement in which corridors are minimized has become popular in many professional offices.

RELOCATION

There are a variety of reasons why a move to a new location may be necessary. First, the conduction of an annual trade area analysis may have shown some changes in the composition of the trade area. For example, many of the clients being served may be relocating and it may now be inconvenient for them to continue to use the professional's service. Further, perhaps the population growth in the trade area is negative which will impact on the pool of clients from which to draw. Another reason for a move is the fact that the practice has outgrown the current space. Simple lack of space may be compromising the ability to deliver quality service to clients. Finally, perhaps it would be wise financially to make a move now if an opportunity for better space arises. Often new building developments offer incentives to secure tenants early in the development stage and it may be possible to capitalize on such an opportunity. In this situation, it is important to conduct a trade area and site assessment for the new location. Depending on the distance from the existing location, it may be possible to retain existing clients and add to the client base in the new location.

Opening a second facility must be done only when appropriate research has been completed. Careful trade area analysis must be undertaken to determine revenue potential and to ensure that no cannibalization of the first facility will occur. If multisite expansion is an option, other factors must also be considered. For example, is there sufficient time to service the new location or will it be necessary to add additional personnel? Is the current location running at capacity, has growth peaked, or can the practice be built up? These decisions are often difficult to make and it may be advisable to seek assistance from other qualified professionals.

SUMMARY

1. The location of a professional services operation is an important consideration. A trade area can be defined as a region where the client may find it reasonable to consume the service or where the service can be delivered economically. Perhaps more importantly, it can be defined as the area where the bulk of business is derived.

2. When searching for a business location, the professional services marketer must consider: (1) the characteristics of the population in the trade area; (2) economic factors; and (3) factors that contribute to the quality of life for those that live and work in the area.

3. When assessing a trade area it is also critical to consider the size of the target market in the trade area and the amount of competition.

4. A professional should be able to calculate the market potential of a trade area by finding out per capita spending on the professional service(s) in the trade area and by multiplying this by the size of the population in the trade area.

5. To determine market share potential, many professionals use the natural market share rule. That is, they divide the total market by the total number of competitors (including themselves) to arrive at an average share. However, rarely does natu-

ral market share occur. Some professionals can achieve more or less depending on their competitive advantage.

6. Several factors determine the exact size and shape of a given trade area. One is the type of professional service; specialized services have a larger trade area. Another is the degree of price competition; consumers may travel farther for better pricing. The number of substitutes or competitors also affects trade area size and finally, physical or psychological barriers affect the size and shape of a trade area.

7. When conducting a trade area analysis on an existing business, the professional services marketer needs to determine: (1) the market potential in the trade area; (2) whether or not it is growing or shrinking; (3) what the current market share is and whether or not it is getting bigger or smaller; (4) where the clients are coming from and how far they travel; and (5) if another site can be opened that will serve new clients not currently using the existing site.

8. A simple way to prepare a trade area analysis is to randomly select 400 client files and to plot on a map where they live or work. This should reveal where the bulk of the clients are drawn from.

9. Once a general trade area is selected, a specific site needs to be chosen. Many of the factors used for trade area analysis come into play for site selection. But other factors include appeal of the site, parking facilities, traffic patterns, zoning regulations, site accessibility, compatibility of neighboring businesses, and the cost and potential of the site.

10. It is also prudent to examine the history of the site and conditions in the immediate area surrounding the site.

11. The physical environment should make the client feel safe and comfortable as well as communicate a sense of the professional's pride in the operation. It should also reflect the quality of professional services that the client should expect.

12. A professional needs to consider the ergonomics and atmo-

spherics of the physical environment. They include: (1) lighting; (2) acoustics; (3) temperature; (4) music; (5) color; and (6) patterns of movement in the space.

13. Physical relocation of an operation may be a consideration for a professional during his or her career. A cost-benefit analysis must be undertaken to determine the feasibility of such a move.

14. It may be advisable to seek professional assistance when conducting a trade area analysis, site assessment, or when considering a move to a new location.

REFERENCE

Stern, Louis W. and Adel I. El-Ansany. *Marketing Channels*, Englewood Cliffs, N.J.: Prentice-Hall, 2nd ed., 1982.

Chapter Eight

Communication — The Key to Success in Professional Services Marketing

Much of a professional's time is actually spent communicating to clients and employees. Because of the intangibility of professional services, consumers often have difficulty judging quality of service. Often the only way to convey quality is to communicate it to the client. A professional's performance is often based on how well he or she can communicate. However, there have been many recent studies that suggest many professionally trained people suffer from poor communication and interpersonal skills. What this means is that there are many technically competent professionals who will not be successful in business simply because of their inability to communicate with clients and employees.

Chapter Four referred to the concept of functional quality in professional services marketing. A major component of functional quality is the ability of the professional to convey care and concern to the client (as well as the employee). While a professional may be caring and concerned he or she must be able to communicate it effectively to the clients. Improving communication skills can improve the chances of success in professional services marketing. Remember while clients may be buying a service from the professional, they are actually buying the professional. Because of inseparability, the professional and client must come together to create the service exchange; as such the professional is an integral part of the service. Satisfying clients' needs will be dependent on how well the professional can communicate with the client before, during, and after the exchange process.

BARRIERS TO COMMUNICATION

Barriers to effective communication between the client and professional are many and varied. There is a tremendous opportunity for miscomprehension and misunderstanding during every contact with a client. Some of the most important variables that can create barriers to effective communication are:

1. *Language* — Professional terminology or jargon can confuse and intimidate clients.
2. *Ego* — Often clients have difficulty accepting the fact that they need help and may become ego-defensive. This may create a barrier for effective communication. Conversely, the professional's ego may get in the way when a client asks a question, or states an objection about the instructions or advice. Thus, the professional may fail to listen effectively.
3. *Level of Knowledge* — Sometimes there is an assumption that a client has a certain level of knowledge about the problem or solution under consideration. This assumption may lead to providing too little information.
4. *Negative Attitudes* — A client can enter the purchase situation with a negative attitude about the professional or the profession. A bad previous experience can be the reason for the negative attitude and thus the client may put up a protective barrier which can inhibit communication.
5. *One-Way Communication* — This is the case where the professional talks and the client listens. With no feedback from

the client, the chances of miscomprehension occurring for either party is high.

CHARACTERISTICS OF GOOD COMMUNICATORS

In Chapter Six one of the fundamentals of management was Fundamental #3 "Be a communications specialist." But what makes a good communicator? Here are several attributes that characterize good communicators:

1. *Confidence* — Good communicators convey confidence. Professionals have to gain the trust of their clients and one key way to do so is to communicate confidence. The image projected can increase the professional's credibility in the eyes of his or her clients. Clients who are confident in you will help maintain and enhance your confidence in yourself. There are several things you can do to communicate confidence: (1) have the right professional appearance; (2) always be prepared; and (3) use a strong clear tone when speaking.
2. *Sincerity* — Good communicators are able to demonstrate sincerity and conviction when they speak. Since many clients are relying on the professional's skills, advice, and guidance, they want to be reassured that he or she is sincere and believes strongly in what he or she is conveying.
3. *Thoroughness* — Clients expect that professionals will offer thorough service. Some professionals may offer such thoroughness but may fail to communicate it to their clients. They must tangibilize their thoroughness through proper communication with the client. They should walk clients through the service procedure orally in order to show them that time and care has been taken in dealing with their problem. The key here is to focus on important points (the things

the client wants to know) and be sure to cover those points completely.

4. *Friendliness* — People with good communication skills are capable of projecting friendliness. A professional that can project an image of friendliness will have a competitive advantage over one that cannot. Clients demand courteous professional service but prefer to deal with professionals who are friendly. This friendliness is important in relationship building. A professional may be a friendly person but can have difficulty communicating it. Often professionals seek to deal with clients with professional detachment. However, a client is a human being and can, at times, be scared, anxious, or stressed about their problem. Friendliness on the part of the professional can ease the stress the client may be feeling when consuming a professional service.

5. *Simplicity* — A key characteristic of good communicators is the ability to converse in a simple and direct way. Often professionals fall into the trap of overwhelming their clients with complex responses or endless use of jargon. They should communicate with clients in a direct and simple manner. If professional terminology is used, explanations in laypersons' language is required so that the client will know what the terms mean.

6. *Listening* — Maybe the most important characteristic of a good communicator is solid listening skills. In order to solve a client's problem and offer reasonable advice, the professional needs to truly understand the client's problem. Only through effective listening can the professional get to the crux of the problem.

If one can communicate with confidence, sincerity, thoroughness, friendliness, and simplicity and practice the art of listening, one will be communicating care and concern for clients. This ability may be one of the most important parts of a competitive arsenal.

NONVERBAL COMMUNICATION

While some professionals have mastered verbal communications, many have not considered the impact of nonverbal communications when dealing with clients. Many researchers believe that nonverbal communication plays a more important role in interpersonal communication. In fact, research indicates that nonverbal messages account for as much as sixty-seven to ninety percent of the total meaning produced in face-to-face communication. Nonverbal communication can be used to reinforce verbal communication or can mitigate or contradict the verbal message.

Virtually anything other than verbal communication, including the way words are used, can be considered nonverbal communication. Nonverbal communication occurs simultaneously with much of verbal communication and can include paralinguistic phenomena (how something is said), posture, walk, gestures, handshake, spacing, and facial expression.

Nonverbal communication can occur in the absence of verbal communication through symbols, as well as through social and physical cues (clues), and the structure of the overall environment. The importance of impression management as a major component of a client management program has already been discussed in Chapter Four. The importance of the physical and social environment (e.g., the nonverbal messages created by the appearance and dress of the professional, the physical surroundings, etc.) surrounding the professional service was covered. Here the focus will be on nonverbal communication as it pertains to paralinguistic phenomena, posture, walk, gestures, hand-shake, spacing, and facial expression.

Paralinguistic Phenomena

This includes the voice pitch, speed, volume, and use of words. The manner of speaking provides meaning to what is said. Obviously, a good voice is a requirement for good communication. Voice should not hinder the message. Monotone voices do not hold the attention of listeners, so a variation in pitch is required. Determining how fast to speak is another consideration. Generally, professionals should present the easy parts of the message at a fast pace and the more difficult parts at a slower rate. The correct use of pauses is also important. Frequent pausing can be irritating but properly placed pauses can emphasize certain material and gain attention. Obviously, one must speak loudly enough for clients to hear but one should not speak too loudly. Varying voice volume helps create interest and emphasis. Giving words their proper meaning and emphasis can be accomplished by varying pitch, speed, and volume.

What words are used is also an important part of nonverbal communication. It has already been suggested that it is important to verbally communicate with simple, short words when dealing with clients and to avoid professional jargon. But the use of words also carries a nonverbal message. For example, not only may clients misunderstand if a complicated vocabulary is used, but nonverbally they may also get the impression that the professional is trying to overpower or intimidate them.

Posture

This is one thing that a client is very apt to notice about the professional. Even clients not close enough to see facial expressions will still see the general form of the body. Professionals should keep their body erect without appearing too stiff. They should always avoid looking too limp. Their posture should convey that they are alert, confident, and communicative. They should try to appear natural, not artificial. They need to ask others to give them feedback on posture and if improvement is suggested, then practice is in order.

Walk

Clients can form an impression simply by the way the professional walks. A strong, brisk, and confident walk is appropriate. A hesitant or awkward walk should not be used since it can convey a negative nonverbal message to the client.

Handshake

The author was once told by a consumer that a professional's handshake was the signal to his or her character. This consumer would not use a dentist with a weak handshake because it conveyed a wimpy or insecure personality. Conversely, this consumer would avoid a lawyer with a bonecrushing handshake because it conveyed an overbearing personality. A professional should use a handshake that demonstrates confidence and caring. A good handshake takes practice and should never be underestimated as a nonverbal communicator.

Spacing

Crossculturally there are significant differences in acceptable distances between speakers. For professionals in the U.S. and Canada, research has indicated that standing or sitting about three feet apart is the optimal distance for effective communication to occur. Being too close may make the client uncomfortable, while being too far away from a client sends a nonverbal message that perhaps the professional does not care.

Facial Expression

Harrison (1976) suggests that "the face is perhaps our most powerful nonverbal communicator" (p. 217). Mehrabian (1972) has gone further by arguing that 55 percent of interpersonal communication is via facial expression. So, the saying "it was written all over his or her face" has an important meaning for professionals. They can tell clients they care but if clients do not see it in their faces, then it is not believable. Often professionals are unconscious about the use of facial expressions and can, unwittingly, convey unintended messages. While certain facial expressions convey different meanings crossculturally, a smile and a frown have universal meaning. As mentioned in Chapter Four, clients demand courteous professionals but prefer friendly professionals. A smiling face is a cue to friendliness.

An important part of facial expression is the use of the eyes. The eyes, long considered the mirrors of the soul, demonstrate to the client whether or not one is caring and sincere. Eye contact is an important part of the communications process between clients and professionals. Maintaining good eye contact with clients provides them with a positive nonverbal message. It clearly shows that professionals are interested and respect them.

COMMUNICATION BY TYPE OF PERSONNEL IN PROFESSIONAL SERVICES MARKETING

Obviously, it has been argued here that effective communication, verbally and nonverbally, plays a central role in the delivery of professional services. Professional services marketers need to improve their knowledge of the communication process, identify the types of communication exchanges that occur with clients, and train personnel to be competent in those specific communication exchanges.

In the professional services environment, communications with clients can range from very simple to very complex exchange processes. Booms and Nyquist (1981) have developed a classification schema that shows the communication requirements demanded by particular positions in service organizations. In essence, personnel in the service environment can be categorized based on the communication demands placed on them by the client. Booms and Nyquist suggest there are three different types of jobs or people in the services organization. These authors also provide the type of communication skills and techniques that are required by each type of job.

Type #1

People in this position must deal effectively with brief, often frequent, and one-time only communication interactions with many clients. Communication usually involves the exchange of simple and limited amounts of information. An effective communicator in this job category must be able to process short, rapid messages quickly and provide a limited number of appropriate responses to consumer inquiries. They must avoid treating clients like objects and being treated like objects themselves. Clear concise instruction skills are required as well as solid listening ability. The ability to defuse anger and establish client rapport quickly is also necessary. An example of a person or job that fits the Type #1 category is the receptionist in a professional office.

Type #2

The communications involved in this type of job consists of restricted interactions with clients but will be longer in duration than those in Type #1. The information exchanged can vary from the simple to the more complex and this job requires more independent decision making. An effective communicator in this job category requires effective listening skills, and an ability to provide clear instructions. It also requires an ability to establish trust, good interpretation skills and the ability to persuade. The relationship between the client and employee is ongoing and the flow of information more intense. An example of a person or job that fits in Type #2 is a paralegal in a legal office, a nurse in a physician's office, or a dental hygienist in a dental office.

Type #3

Positions in this category require the most complex communication skills of all. Communication involves repeated interactions with the client over time and includes an extensive flow of information. The communication tasks in this category are complicated and often nonrepeatable. To be effective in this category requires strong listening skills, the ability to process complicated information, and the skill of asking appropriate questions. Abilities to express feelings, make decisions quickly, and think creatively in a one-to-one setting are required. Examples of people or jobs that fall into Type #3 are lawyers, physicians, accountants, and other high-contact professional services suppliers.

Most professional services firms will have personnel in one, two, or all three categories. The key for professional services marketers is to understand that the client often requires a broad range of communications and that personnel dealing with clients need specific communication competencies. In order to successfully communicate with clients, the professional services marketer needs to:

1. Identify the types of client and personnel communication exchanges that occur.

2. Consider the appropriate type of communication responses that are necessary for the various personnel in the firm.
3. Hire personnel with the communication competencies for the job.
4. Train personnel in specific communication competencies.
5. Develop communication policies and procedures to facilitate effective communication.

INTERNAL COMMUNICATIONS

It has been argued that employees should be treated like clients. As such, internal communication is just as important as client communication. In order to ensure that quality of service is maintained in a professional services environment, two cornerstones need to be put in place:

1. Employees should know exactly what the professional's role is, and precisely their role in client management. What everyone is to do and say when dealing with clients should be spelled out well.
2. Everyone should regularly exchange information concerning all aspects of client contact.

As was shown in Chapter Five, one of the fundamentals of management is the ability to provide clear and concise directions about what needs to be accomplished in a professional setting. Asking for feedback from employees about the given assignments is also critical. Ensuring effective internal communication requires an open and honest environment that fosters such communication. One thing that can help is to conduct a five- to ten-minute minimeeting every day before the day begins to discuss the priorities of the day, and to review the previous day's activities. It is essential to keep these minimeetings short. If a major problem is aired, set aside another time to handle it but assure employees that it will be dealt with. In addition to "as required" meetings that may be necessary to handle such problems, a professional practice should hold either a regular weekly or monthly meeting. It can be used to discuss practice policies and procedures, staffing requirements, business development ideas, or suggestion exchanges. Be certain that an agenda is prepared and that everyone has the opportunity for input.

CLIENT COMPLAINTS

Recent research has shown that for every complaint a business receives, there are twenty-six others that feel the same way but whose complaints are not aired (*Marketing News*, 1991). This means the possibility of twenty-six lost clients per every complaint received. This has serious implications to professionals since it has already been learned in Chapter Four that it costs five times as much to replace a client as it does to retain one. It also means that using numbers of complaints received as a measure of client satisfaction or service quality can be very misleading.

Why is it that clients do not complain directly to professionals? The primary reason is because, culturally, complaint behavior has not been accepted as an integral part of the marketing system. It is just not very appropriate to complain! Most people fear that others will view them as chronic complainers even if there are legitimate reasons for their dissatisfaction. Moreover, most organizations tend to exacerbate the problem by discouraging, not encouraging, complaint behavior. Employees in particular do not want to bring forth client complaints to the organizations for fear of reprisal by management. Complaints are not viewed as fundamental feedback. Some consumer research shows that when clients are asked about why they do not complain, rarely does this cultural dimension surface. However, clients do say that the reasons for not complaining include (1) a feeling of helplessness (it wouldn't make any difference) and (2) a feeling that it would not be worth the time and effort. Under the surface of these responses lies the fact that a client feels uncomfortable challenging a professional who is paid for his or her expertise. Also, the service encounter is now complete and cannot be re-called, so complaining after the fact is viewed as an exercise in futility. Therefore, the concept of voting with their feet works best for most clients. They do not complain, they just do not come back.

However, what about those who do take the time and effort to complain? What is the basis for the majority of complaints these clients have about professional services providers? Chapter Four showed that one of the main things consumers want from profes-sionals is care and concern. It should not come as a surprise that the number one reason for complaints is simply that clients do not believe the professional cares about them.

Many clients, however, do not word their complaints in such an open fashion. Sometimes they put up a smoke screen to hide their true feelings. For example, look at some of the common complaints that the author hears when he conducts his research on consumers' satisfaction/dissatisfaction with professional ser-vices. What the consumer went on to say when probed about their statements is in parentheses.

1. He didn't listen to a thing I said. (He was too busy to care about me.)
2. She treated me like an object. (She didn't care that I was a person.)
3. She never calls me by name. (She obviously doesn't care about me if she can't remember my name.)
4. He always makes me wait. (He doesn't consider me an im-portant client.)

While much research shows that dissatisfaction with services can involve waiting time, inconvenient hours, indifferent treatment, or overcharging, the majority of complaints, at least from this professional's research, can be traced back to the professional's inability to communicate that he or she cares about his or her clients. If poor communication has caused the complaints, countering the complaints will require communication skills. When clients want the professional to recover (make the situation right), he or she needs to communicate effectively in order to remedy the situation. (When dealing with client complaints use the recovery guidelines outlined in Chapter Four, Figure 4-6 on page 59.)

SUMMARY

1. Good communication skills can mean the difference between success and failure in professional services marketing.

2. There are several barriers to communication between a client and a professional. These include: (1) language; (2) ego; (3) level of knowledge; (4) negative attitudes; and (5) one-way communication.

3. There are several attributes that characterize good communicators. They include: (1) confidence; (2) sincerity; (3) thoroughness; (4) friendliness; (5) simplicity; and (6) listening skills.

4. Nonverbal communication may account for sixty-seven to ninety percent of the total meaning produced in face-to-face communication. Professionals need to consider how nonverbal communication affects their verbal communication.

5. Key areas of nonverbal communication that the professional must master are: (1) paralinguistic phenomena (how something is said); (2) posture; (3) walk; (4) gestures; (5) handshake; (6) spacing; and (7) facial expression.

6. Research suggests that there are three different types of jobs or people involved in the communications process with cli-

ents. They are classified as Type #1, Type #2 and Type #3. Each requires different communications skills.

7. In order to successfully communicate with clients, the professional services marketer needs to: (1) identify the types of communication exchanges that occur in their environment; (2) consider the communication responses that are necessary for personnel in the firm; (3) hire personnel with the communication competencies for the job; (4) train personnel in communication competencies; and (5) develop policies and procedures for effective communication.

8. It is important for professional services marketers to have good internal communications. An environment that fosters good communication between individuals in the organization is vital. Everyone should know their role in client contact relations and regular and ongoing exchanges of information within the organization must be encouraged.

9. Research shows that only 1 in 27 clients complain about the service they receive. This is a serious problem since it means clients are voting with their feet and running from the business rather than staying to complain.

10. Generally clients do not complain because culturally we do not encourage complaint behavior. Also, clients feel helpless or feel it would not do any good to complain.

11. When they do complain, however, the number one reason is because they do not feel the professional cares about them. They may mask the complaint, but behind the screen is the feeling that the professional does not care.

12. When a client complains, he or she must be taken seriously and the professional must recover from the situation. Using the recovery guidelines in Chapter Four is an important part of the process.

13. Communicating care and concern can be the most important part of your competitive advantage; use it.

REFERENCES

Booms, Bernard H. and Jody L. Nyquist. "Analyzing the Customer/Firm Communication Component of the Services Marketing Mix," in *Marketing of Services*, James H. Donnelly and William R. George (eds.), Chicago: American Marketing Association, 1981, pp. 172-177.

Harrison, R. P. "The Face in Face-to-Face Communication," in De Sola Pool and W. Schramm (eds.), *Handbook of Communication*, New York: Rand McNally, 1976.

Marketing News, "Satisfaction-Action to Offer Tips on Pleasing Customers," February 4, 1991, p. 4.

Mehrabian, A. *Nonverbal Communication*, Chicago: Aldine-Atherton, 1972.

Chapter Nine

Professional Services Marketing in the Future

No one knows for sure what is in store for professionals in the future, not even futurist gurus. But the author feels that the professional services market in the next 10-15 years should be characterized by intense competitive pressure as a result of lower entry barriers and a lack of population growth. Quite simply, too many professionals will be serving too few consumers. There will be very few underdeveloped markets, including geographically rural areas. This saturation will lead to even more aggressive promotion as the professional services sector goes through the late maturity stage of its life cycle. However, heavy promotion may not be the solution for many professional services firms. Many will have to rethink their approach to business. Market share management will be the key. Holding on to clients and securing dissatisfied clients from competitors will be the only ways to achieve growth. Emphasis will be placed on the functional quality aspects of service, such as care and empathy for clients, in order to achieve a competitive advantage. As professional services firms become even more marketing-oriented, there will be a greater emphasis on increasing profit margins instead of sales volume. Cost reduction strategies will also be emphasized. There will continue to be much concern over professional liability, not strictly because of the costs of litigation and awards, but because of the public perception created as a result of such activities.

Education about marketing as a process and philosophy will become an inherent part of the professional arena. Universities who train professionals will include courses in their curriculum on marketing and business management. Continuing education and ongoing professional development in these areas will be required in many states and provinces. The use of research to define and understand target markets and to measure service performance will become commonplace. There will be greater emphasis on the recruitment of service-oriented professionals and staff as opposed to strictly technically competent personnel. Planning, both short term and long term, will be built into the fabric of professional services firms.

While this book has offered some market predictions and the responses that may be or will be required by professionals, what else will professional services firms have to do to compete effectively in the future? Any professional hoping to maintain and expand market share in the future will need to consider the following:

1. Professional services firms will need to apply internal marketing throughout their organization. Only satisfied employees can deliver client satisfaction. The professional services organization must buy into marketing in order to use it effectively. In the future, management methods, procedures, personnel policies, training, and feedback must all be geared toward the internal marketing concept. Very simply, a professional services firm cannot be client-oriented if it is not employee-oriented.

2. Professionals will need to embrace impression management. Because clients evaluate what they cannot see by what they can see, professional services marketers must manage the tangible evidence surrounding their service. The marketplace will be even more competitive in the future so conveying the appropriate image to the client will become a necessity. Everything that speaks about the service must be integrated, coordi-

nated, and managed, and it must be done better than the competitors.

3. Professional services firms will need to manage service quality; both technical and functional. In the future, service quality may be the only way to create differentiation in a marketplace of homogeneity. Research on the determinants of service quality must be conducted and service quality performance measures must be a regular part of the professional services firm's operation. Functional quality such as care and empathy for clients may be more important to stress in professional services firms, but this does not mean it can compensate for poor technical quality.

4. Professional services marketers must stress relationship marketing in order to ensure growth. Getting to know clients well and being able to cater specifically to their needs will be critical in the future. Servicing and marketing to existing clients must be considered as important as acquiring new clients. Relationship marketing should be viewed as a "cultivation process," a way to ensure repeat business. Greater involvement with the client will lead to client loyalty.

5. Professionals must practice synchromarketing. Idle capacity is, and will be, a problem with professional services marketing in the future. But, perhaps more difficult will be the inability to handle peak load demand. The synchronizing of demand and supply must be a priority in the future.

6. Professional services marketers will need to develop a systems approach to service excellence. This must include a well-defined strategy, good people to deliver the service, and a flexible and responsive service structure to support the people serving the client. Finding a competitive advantage, or doing what you do best, and doing it better than your competitors will be fundamental in the future. Hiring, training, and motivating employees to put the client first will also be crucial. A service system must

be designed that meets the needs of both the employee and the client. The system must be structured around the convenience of the client and not the professional.

7. Professionals will have to consider greater use of paraprofessionals in order to keep operating costs down and to increase productivity. As long as these personnel are competent, client-driven, and deployed effectively, their use should be encouraged.

8. Professionals will need to balance high tech and high touch. In the pursuit of greater productivity, many firms will use technology to standardize or industrialize professional services. Many firms will go too far and abandon the personal touch. This should be avoided. While technology should and must be used, professional services firms are in the people business and clients must not be dehumanized in the exchange process.

9. Professionals will need to manage information more efficiently. Information will be an important part of a successful professional practice in the future. Professionals will need to have an integrated information management system including an expert system and/or artificial intelligence component as well as a comprehensive database system for client management.

10. Professionals will need to recognize the concept of segmented market growth. Overall, the market will be mature and exhibit slow growth but some segments will offer greater potential than others. Key segments to watch will be the seniors markets and to a lesser extent, the youth market and the professional working women segment.

11. Professionals will need to shift away from price as a competitive edge. While there is and will be a market for the professional who seeks the price-sensitive consumer, this market is ever shifting and offers little room for relationship marketing. A larger and more important market will consist of the better edu-

cated and professional consumer, or the smart shopper, who will be a cornerstone of the professional services market in the future. They will be seeking quality, value, and an ongoing relationship with their professionals. For this market, price is but one attribute to consider when buying professional services.

12. Professional services firms will need to manage client satisfaction. Client retention will be the key to growth in the future and thus client satisfaction should become the number one priority in professional services firms. By employing internal marketing, impression management, relationship marketing, synchromarketing, and managing service quality, the professional services marketer can ensure client satisfaction in the future.

In conclusion, professionals must recognize that wearing a professional's hat also brings with it the responsibility of wearing a businessperson's hat. The two are not incompatible, in fact, they are inextricably linked. For professional service suppliers, becoming marketing-oriented will be a fundamental prerequisite to survival and prosperity in the future. There should be no future debate over whether or not marketing has a place in professional services. Rather, the issue will be how to effectively and ethically market professional services so that both the professional and the consumer can benefit. In the future, when a professional dons a business hat, it should and must be the one with the marketing label attached to it.

Index